LAWYERS, GUBS AND MONKEYS

Lawyers, Gubs and Monkeys

William W. Bedsworth

Editing: Nelson P. Miller
Illustrations: Robin Crossman
Typesetting and cover design: Anita Jovanovic

Published by:

 Vandeplas Publishing, LLC – November 2015

801 International Parkway, 5th Floor
Lake Mary, FL. 32746
USA

www.vandeplaspublishing.com

ISBN 978-1-60042-275-1

LAWYERS, GUBS AND MONKEYS

WILLIAM W. BEDSWORTH

For Bill, Megan, and Cait
Take heart; I'm only half the gene pool

I was gambling in Havana, I took a little risk,
Send lawyers, guns and money; Dad, get me out of this.

Warren Zevon, "Lawyers, Guns, and Money"

Holdup note: "Please put 50,000 dollars into this bag and act natural.
I'm pointing a gun at you."
Bank Teller: What does this say?
Holdup man (Woody Allen): I'm pointing a gun at you.
Bank Teller: That looks like "gub"; that doesn't look like "gun".
Holdup man: No, it's gun.
Bank Teller: No, it's "gub"; that's a "b".
Holdup man: No, see, that's an "n". Gun.
Bank Teller calls over second teller who agrees with Woody that the
questioned word is "gun" but wants to know what "abt natural" means.
Things go downhill precipitously, and Woody does not get the $50,000.

Woody Allen, Take the Money and Run

The Judicial Wisdom of the Year Award goes to Justice William Bedsworth
for recognizing that, "There is no non-culpable explanation for monkeys in
your underpants."

Times of London, 2004

TABLE OF CONTENTS

Dedication   v

Table of Contents   vii

Foreword   ix

Introduction   xi

As a reader of this book, you will smile a lot, laugh out loud occasionally, and learn a great deal. The book is a collection of columns that were written by California Court of Appeal Justice William Bedsworth. They are humorous essays of a sort rarely found any more and we are all worse for that. I remember reading Art Buchwald for years and his wry observations on our political system and current events. Justice Bedsworth – commonly referred to by many, including him, as Beds – is a worthy successor to Buchwald and writes in a similar style. The essays are written in the first person, meant to be amusing, and are his observations on law and life and the world. They were initially penned as columns titled, "A Criminal Waste of Space," his award-winning, nationally-syndicated column. But they read wonderfully as a book of short essays and are anything but a waste of space.

The columns cover topics ranging from the amount Medicare spends on penis pumps, to Pakistan banning words like "gonzaga" and "monkey crotch" on the internet, to the value of Zimbabwean currency, to the failure of Justice Clarence Thomas to ask questions at oral arguments in the United States Supreme Court. Most are not about law, even though they are written by a judge, but some touch on legal issues and his experiences on the bench.

Many of the essays are of the type that a comic like Jerry Seinfeld would use as a monologue. Beds takes life experiences or things in the news and does a riff on them. He tells of his experience in having a bank telling him that a newly opened account is closed in a manner that is entertaining and that all of us can relate to. His column on interactive urinal cakes – yes, urinal cakes that speak to men at the urinal – is hilarious. But it has a serious side too: their use in Colorado has decreased driving while intoxicated arrests by 10%. He has a column on Romania adopting a tax on witches and an intellectual property lawsuit in Australia about a company that wanted to call its product, "Nucking Futs."

The columns that touch on the law are written with the same light touch and will be enjoyed by non-lawyers and lawyers alike. But they make some thoughtful points. He has a terrific column on arbitration clauses in form contracts and the inability of consumers and employees to do anything about them. I particularly enjoyed his column on why he asks questions from the bench in oral argument and the reasons for different types of judges' inquiries.

Along the way, we learn a great deal about Beds. He is a baseball fan and a pet lover and is clearly skeptical of politicians of all persuasions, though has a grudging admiration of them too. He was a prosecutor and an NHL official and a trial judge before becoming a court of appeal justice in 1997. We learn a bit about his wife Kelly and occasionally his children and grandchildren. Most of all, what comes through in the essays is a warm, often self-deprecating humorist who enjoys his life and wants to share his observations about it.

These are the type of essays that a Mark Twain or a James Thurber would write and it made me realize how rare it is to find this kind of writing any more. There is one important difference, though, from other essays of this type: Beds' columns have footnotes. Be sure and read the footnotes, they are often hilarious.

Erwin Chemerinsky

There is no greater engine on the face of the planet for doing good than the American legal system. It is serious stuff and it requires serious people. If you aren't ready to give it everything you've got every time out, you should find something else to do with your life.

But most of us aren't wired to give full amperage all day, every day. You try to force that kind of voltage through your system every day, you're gonna spend a lot of time putting out electrical fires and replacing conduit. Human beings need to shut down and reset the mechanism every so often.

Fun resets the mechanism.

I write these as a way of hitting the reset button. Appellate law does not provide any equivalent button. There's not much funny about the cases that reach our court. You can't laugh at a prison sentence, and nobody wants to read, "Your ten million dollar judgment is reversed . . . but did you hear the one about the nun and the parrot and the sailor?"

Fortunately, life is full of weird, quirky stuff, much of which finds its way to the courts. And a life in the law provides *plenty* of material for laughter. Within these covers are a few years worth of my musings – mostly bemused, always amused – on the law, the legal profession, and the many "He did WHAT??!!" moments that allow me to reset and prepare for the next case.

I hope they'll make you laugh. They should give you a better grasp of some seldom discussed legal concepts like The Doctrine of Unintended Consequences and The Canon of Relative Filth. Who knows, they may even keep your wiring from overheating.

William W. Bedsworth

"Gods and Godlings"

"AN OBSCURE FEDERAL CASE MAY EXPLAIN A LOT."

Pay attention. This column is actually going to have some redeeming social value. Not a whole lot, but some. Get ready.

I want you to read this sentence, from a published opinion of the Ninth Circuit Court of Appeals, and tell me what about it strikes you as unusual – unusual, that is, even for the Ninth Circuit:

"We believe the controlling issue, however, is whether, as of the time of the publication, the Foundation, the copyright claimant, could trace its title back to the humans who owned the original common law copyright."

You done? All right, what struck you as unusual about that sentence? No, no, besides the six commas.

How about the use of the word, "humans." When's the last time you read an opinion in which a court found it necessary to describe the legal position of the "humans?"

Let me just suggest to you that any time you find a court referring to participants in a lawsuit as "humans," you've found yourself an opinion that is not going to be just another roadside attraction. The only reason for referring to the holders of the original copyright as "humans" is to differentiate them from the NON-HUMANS. That's pretty much my definition of a case worth reading.[1]

Which, of course, pretty much assures that it's going to end up with the feds. They get all the really good alien being, spaceship sighting, Elvis is alive and well and working for the CIA in my rec room kind of cases. That's because, under a little-known federal law, they get first choice.

And, of course, the Ninth Circuit gets first choice of all the goofy cases that come out of California, Nevada and Arizona. That's like having a license to mine gold in Fort Knox. I mean, between the half-baked ideas that come out of California and the over-cooked ideas that come out of the desert southwest, the Ninth Circuit gets to listen to more craziness than Mick Jagger's therapist. For example, they get cases like *Urantia Foundation v. Maaherra.*

Here[2] are the UNCONTESTED facts of *Urantia Foundation v. Maaherra,* 114 F.3d 955. I took these right out of the court's opinion. Read them and tell me you wouldn't be bitter if the Ninth Circuit kept stealing cases like this from you.

---

1   Which, as my colleagues on the Court of Appeal are wont to explain to me, is not the standard for publication set forth in rule 976(b) of the California Rules of Court. Pity.

2   Well, not RIGHT "here." Starting with the next paragraph "here." You've gotta give me time to introduce them. This writing stuff is a lot tougher than it looks.

According to the Ninth Circuit, the Urantia Book is a collection of divine revelations, authored by "non-human spiritual beings" including the Divine Counselor, the Chief of the Archangels of Nebadon, and, my personal favorite, the Chief of the Corps of Superuniverse Personalities.

Wouldn't you just love to be the Chief of the Corps of Superuniverse Personalities? I mean, just being a Superuniverse Personality would be really cool. But being the chief of the entire corps, THAT would be a great job.

How many Superuniverse Personalities do you suppose there are? I mean, I figure Dr. Phil is pretty obviously one of them. And John Tesh. Arianna Huffington, maybe. But beyond that, I think they've done an admirable job of cloaking their identities.[3]

Perhaps too good. The revelations of the Superuniverse Personalities *et al.* were divulged through – I am not making this up – the "patient of a Chicago psychiatrist." The Chicago psychiatrist is identified by the Ninth Circuit only as "Dr. Sadler." The name of the patient who actually walked into Dr. Sadler's office with the stone tablets in tow is not divulged, presumably due to patient/psychotherapist privilege.

Isn't it always the way? I mean, if the godhead would just make these pronouncements through the President of the United States or the Speaker of the House of Representatives or Stephen Colbert, or somebody else we all believe all the time, the whole religion thing would be a lot easier. But She keeps picking people with very little credibility ... like psychiatrists. This really seems an unnecessary complication of stuff that's already tough enough.

And before I go any further into this, let me hasten to point out I am NOT disparaging anyone's religious beliefs. Do not send me letters about religious intolerance. Most of my family are Zen Golf-Baptists: They believe dancing is sinful unless you do it in sand and rake up your footprints.

---

3   Unlike the Archangels of Nebadon, who, if I'm not mistaken, are the Double-A farm club of the Cincinnati Reds and finished 13 games out of first place in the Carolina League this season.

I myself happen to belong to a religion that accepts as fact burning bushes which speak and people who live inside the bellies of large fishes for extended periods of time. My religion is just chock full of stuff Isaac Newton and Steven Hawking on their best days couldn't make heads nor tails of. Having bought into all of that, I am in no position to indulge in religious bigotry.

Besides, I really know nothing about what these people believe except that it involves a whole crew of archangels I never heard of, and that doesn't bother me a bit. Near as I can determine every religion gets to name its own archangels, just as every major league manager gets to name his own coaches. Seems fair to me. I figure until one of these groups shows up with a notarized document from God, we're free to root for whatever team we want. I lose very little sleep over OTHER people's religious beliefs.

I am, however, seriously frosted about what terrific cases other courts get. I have nothing against the Ninth Circuit – which, as I understand it, disqualifies me for Congress, but that's not a bad deal, either – I just don't understand why they merit this case, while highly-qualified deep-thinkers like me plod through the muck of cases involving mere mortals. Why should a court that spends most of its time struggling to get its batting average above the Mendoza line get thrown softballs like this one?

But I digress.

To return to the actual reported decision – a fact which I mention here because I think it's easy to lose sight of the fact that this isn't satire, it's MCLE – Dr. Sadler did what anyone would do when confronted with divine revelation: he formed a committee. He got together "five or six followers, called the Contact Commission."

Personally, I think this was a mistake. I haven't had a lot of truck with commissions in my life, but it seems to me they're always riling folks up. Think about it; you got your Securities and Exchange Commission, your Public Utilities Commission, your police commission, your Warren Commission, and all you ever hear about is how unhappy people are with them. I think any chance you have NOT to form a commission should be taken advantage of, but Dr. Sadler did not ask my advice.[4]

According to the Ninth Circuit, "[A]pparently in response to what they perceived to be prompting from the spiritual beings, and in collaboration with a larger group of followers called the Forum, the Contact Commission began to pose specific questions to the spiritual beings. The answers to these questions, as transmitted to the humans and arranged by them, became the Urantia Papers [also known as 'the Book,' the subject of this lawsuit]." 114 F.3d 955, 957. Honest.

Things apparently went well at first. Oh, there was the occasional lawsuit brought by covetous *non-Nebadonians* (see, e.g., *Urantia Foundation v. Burton*, 210 U.S.P.Q. 217 (W.D. Mich. 1980)), and the occasional problem with state courts rejecting believers' freedom-of-religion defenses to their pot-cultivation charges (see, e. g., *People v. Mullins* (1975) 50 Cal.App.3d 61), but nothing more than you'd expect whenever the Divine Counselor is involved.

Until 1990. That's when the folks in charge of the Urantia Book found out someone was distributing it – along with a "study aid," no less[5] – on computer disks. FOR FREE!!

They tracked down defendant Maaherra[6] in Arizona and sued her for infringing the copyright they had presciently obtained in 1956 and renewed in 1983. Her defense was that their copyright was invalid because, after all, THE BOOK WAS NOT WRITTEN BY HUMANS!

This enabled the Ninth Circuit to break some new ground.[7] They noted that "The copyright laws, of course, do not expressly require 'human' authorship ..."[8] but nonetheless upheld the Foundation's claim

---

4   And, when you think about it, if you're dealing with celestial beings, advisory opinions from out-of-state courts are not real high on your "to do" list.

5   Nebadonian Cliffs Notes!

6   Whaddya think? Did they hire a private investigator or just send out for another revelation?

7   This is something they do a lot in the Ninth Circuit. The ground around them must look like a bombing range.

8   Talk about sloppy draftsmanship! How many times do we have to tell Congress to be clearer about which laws apply to the whole universe and which ones apply only to humans?!?!

of copyright violation. This required the pronouncement which is perhaps my favorite thing ever said by a federal judge that did not include dinner plans: "We agree with Maaherra, however, that it is not creations of divine beings that the copyright laws were intended to protect, and that in this case some element of human creativity must have occurred in order for the Book to be copyrightable." 114 F.3d 955, 958.

Tell me if I'm reading too much into it, but isn't that a holding that God has no standing on copyright issues? Isn't the Ninth Circuit hanging out a sign on the area of intellectual property that says, "Divine beings need not apply?"

They make it even clearer later in the paragraph: "At the very least, for a worldly entity to be guilty of infringing a copyright, that entity must have copied something created by another worldly entity." Note they don't say "an other-worldly entity" but "another worldly entity." The other-worldly entities are just S.O.L.[9]

I mean, I don't know where these people worship, but I ordinarily make it a practice to try to decide cases without ruling that DEITIES HAVE NO STANDING! Call me timid, but that just seems real risky to me.

I can only assume the Ninth Circuit has decided the United States Supreme Court is not a sufficiently worthy adversary and has decided to take on the REAL Supreme Court. Talk about tugging on Superman's cape.

I must confess here that I was too timid to Shepardize this case. I wasn't sure whether I'd be more likely to see "Petition granted" or "Plague of locusts visited upon." I'll leave it to you to determine whether *Urantia Foundation v. Maaherra* is still good law.

But you don't need Shepard's to tell you that anybody who rules God has no standing is not a good person to be standing next to during an electrical storm. And, sure enough, of the three judges who joined in this decision, two (Donald P. Lay and Mary M. Schroeder) have been

---

9   This is a fancy technical term the copyright mavens use all the time. I promised you redeeming social value, right?

saddled with the chief judgeship of their respective circuits.[10] And the third, Alfred T. Goodwin, got to decide the Pledge of Allegiance case—not quite a non-stop ticket to hell, but close enough.

So by my lights, none of the godlings who decided this case have been well-treated by the Real Thing since *Urantia*. Just goes to show you, it may take awhile, but the mills of God do not forget. You deny standing to deities, you get ground exceeding small.

---

10 Being C. J. or P. J. of anything strikes me as a fate worse than death. I'd rather be imprisoned in the same cell with a buffalo-molester.

Penis Pumps and Ammo Cans

As a young lawyer, I sometimes made the mistake of envying the savvy of the older guys.[1] This was usually prompted by getting my nose bloodied by someone who had been practicing thirty years and knew how to use his experience against me. I longed for the days when *I* would know where the land mines were and how to lure the opposition into them.

In my naiveté, I imagined a learning process in which you gathered up knowledge in a large ammo can, and then, once it was full, just

---

1   And in those days, they were guys. While my first two supervisors were women (Oretta Sears and Alicemarie Stotler), they were pretty much the only women lawyers I encountered.

reached in and pulled it out when you needed to reload. I figured once I had a full inventory of ammunition, I'd be able to dish it out at the same level at which I was presently taking it.

But it turns out you reach a point where the ammo can is replaced by a sieve. And not only does much of your ammo leak away, you need new and different kinds of ammo because they keep changing the weaponry on you.

I can deal with the legal changes. New issues, new statutes, new technology – they all complicate the job. But every generation of judge faces those problems, and we all learn to pedal a little faster to keep up. There's a webinar next week about the new criminal sentencing scheme and I've signed up for a day-long seminar on family law, an area which seems to generate new problems almost hourly. I'm working to build up my pedaling muscles both literally and figuratively.[2]

But the aging process itself requires me to jam new stuff into my ammo sieve every day. That stuff's harder to keep up with than grandchildren. And it clutters up the sieve; makes it harder to find stuff.

I, for example, have had to make myself an expert on – or at least an aficionado of – arthritis. Much of my youth was misspent as a catcher. A succession of baseball coaches correctly identified me as their most expendable player and assigned me to wear the mask, shin guards, and chest protector sometimes referred to as "the tools of ignorance" (a term I had thought clever and quaint but now recognize as merely an accurate observation).

Catching, it turns out, is slightly worse for your knees than hiring railroad workers to beat on them with a twelve-pound hammer. Even if you're nimble enough to avoid huge base runners charging to the plate,[3] the basic wear and tear of the position turns catchers' orthopedists from boat owners to private plane flyers.

So part of my sieve has to be filled with information about diclofenac and compartmental knee replacement and all kinds of ammo I

---

2   I've installed an exercise bike in chambers.

3   "Nimble" has, unfortunately, never been a part of my repertoire.

had no intention of carrying around when I was envying those older lawyers.

And I'm not even going to start the one-hour lecture I could now deliver on the prostate gland,[4] or my encyclopedic knowledge of the bones of the foot, or any of the other petty indignities of the aging process that now rattle around in my ammo sieve. Suffice it to say I have difficulty understanding how it can keep leaking and still get heavier.

And now I realize I will soon have to learn about Medicare – which, based on my first encounters with it, is a Sanskrit translation of three lost Gospels originally recorded in Etruscan and codified by Axl Rose. I tried to help my dad figure out the prescription drug part of this bureaucratic Grendel a few years back. I developed three ulcers and ran screaming from the room in less than an hour.

Perhaps the obsidian impenetrability of the Medicare Act explains why our government spent 240 million dollars in the last decade buying penis pumps for men my age.

Yep, that's what it says. It says a quarter of a billion dollars for penis pumps. You can read it over and over and it will still say that because it's true.

I was of two minds when I read that number. Part of me said, "I sure hope that's right because if it is, it's a column." Part of me said, "I sure hope that's wrong, because I'm paying those taxes." Part of me just kept shaking its head and saying, "Penis pumps? Really? It's come to that?"

Don't get me wrong. I love sex. My three children will doubtless be disturbed by the information that they were not the only three times I did it.[5] I can fully understand the desire of other members of my gender to attend to this ... urge.

But 240 million dollars? Really? I apologize for what will doubtless seem insensitive to some, but that number calls to mind Jeremy Bentham's phrase "nonsense upon stilts."

---

4   I have suggested to the Presiding Justice that what we need more than another judge is a court urologist.

5   Probably as much as you're disturbed by the glut of information in that paragraph.

Horndog that I am, I still find myself sympathetic to the position of Benjamin Domenech, managing editor of Health Care News, who considers this a "questionable medical need." As John Nothdurft, director of government relations for The Heartland Institute, puts it, "At a time when the federal government borrows 43 cents of every dollar it spends, do we really need to be spending money on this?"[6]

I'll leave the serious analysis of this expenditure to people who actually have some clue what goes on in Medicare.[7] There must be a reason a program that will not pay for eyeglasses or hearing aids will pay for penis pumps.

Yeah, think about that for a minute. Medicare will turn you loose in your automobile when you can't read the numbers on the speedometer or hear a siren. They are apparently unmoved by the prospect you will steer your Buick – blinker frantically signaling a left turn for the last 12 miles because you can't hear it – blindly into a playground you mistook for a parking lot. But the prospect of you being unable to fully enjoy the Playboy Channel has them shelling out 240,000,000 smackdolians.

Call me crazy, but I consider allowing citizens to see and hear a more legitimate government function than making sure they can recreate.[8]

Now before you start that angry email about your father or your neighbor or your cousin Jack, let me hasten to assure you I am prepared to spend tax dollars on penis pumps. I have little doubt there are circumstances in which this is a valid expense.[9]

But a quarter of a billion dollars? Are we having these things hand made by Laguna Beach artisans?

---

6   I should point out that the Health Care News is published by the Heartland Institute. Both of these organizations consider anything left of state-provided roads to be rampant socialism, but in this case I think they may have a point.

7   And however vague that clue might be, it will be several orders of magnitude greater than my own understanding of the topic.

8   And for most men my age, the issue is recreating, not procreating.

9   Although I'd feel a lot better if the folks who needed glasses and hearing aids were in line ahead of the penis-pump recipients.

I mean, how many of them are we buying? The United States Census Bureau estimates there are about 17 million Medicare-age men in the country. Even allowing for the fact there's a lot of turnover in this group, and further allowing for the fact penis pumps are not easily recyclable, so every time one of these men puts in a request, we need a new pump, 240 million seems like a lot of money for this line of the budget.

And it turns out it is. Turns out at least some of that money goes to fraud. Last year an Illinois man pled guilty to buying $26 items on an adult website, repackaging them, and selling them to Medicare penis-pump recipients. He billed the government $284 for each of them. Managed to pocket about two million dollars.

So now my ammo can contains the fact Medicare pays for penis pumps. It contains the fact taxpayers spend about 25 million dollars a year to purchase them for men over the age of 65. It contains the fact there are people in the world who would market fraudulent penis pumps to their country and their fellow man. And it contains the fact there are millions of dollars to be made pumping fraudulent penis pumps.

To make room for that information, I have had to jettison The Rule in Shelley's Case, my understanding of Sections 11116-47000 of the Food and Agriculture Code, the names of three members of the Sixth District Court of Appeal, and the place I left my car keys.

Today's practice tips, therefore, are for young lawyers:

1. It does not get easier.

2. Buy lightweight ammo cans; they can get pretty heavy by the time you're done with them.

THE CURSE OF THE CARBONIC RESERVES

If you're not a baseball fan, you probably think the Colorado Rockies are a place – a mountain range with a state designation appended to distinguish them from the Canadian Rockies or the inexplicably unsung Montana Rockies.[1] If that is your mindset, more power to you. You've avoided one of life's great addictions, a time sink down the drain of which I have poured more of my biblically allotted three-score-and ten than I care to recount.

---

1   Glacier National Park is in the Montana Rockies, and if you're a fan of glaciers, grizzly bears, or gravedigger's ass cold, it's a beauty.

I am a fanatic baseball fan. If I'd had a decent high school guidance counselor, I'd be doing play-by-play for the Albuquerque Isotopes today. Until arthritis took my knees away, my goal in life was to die at the age of 86, trying to go from first to third on a single.

My mom is responsible for this derangement. She got me hooked on baseball. At her funeral, three different friends commented about remembering her playing catch with me in the front yard. Women playing baseball were as alien to fifties life as horses playing clarinet. But Mom loved the game and she loved me. Ergo ....

Dad was not interested. Little League, American Legion, high school, college – I played 'em all and he never saw a game. He was not only uninterested in sports, he was antagonistic. He used to say, "I hate sports the way people who love sports hate common sense."

He seemed to think it was enough he bought the gloves and the bats and the cleats and whatever – applying money that was in very short supply to something he did not approve of. And he was right. He didn't have another level of support in him. He gave me the highest gear he had.

So Mom is to blame for the fact I love baseball with a passion most people reserve for sex objects and money. And it's her fault that you've read this far only to find out the rest of this column is not about the Front Range or the San Juans but the *other* Colorado Rockies: a team in the National League of Professional Baseball Clubs.[2]

The Rockies have to be the only organization in baseball whose lawyers get more work than their bullpen.

It started in 1991. To appreciate that, you need to understand the Rockies were created – much as Michelangelo depicted creation as an old man reaching out his finger – in 1991, when Commissioner of Baseball Fay Vincent reached out his finger and touched a couple of businessmen from Florida and Denver and created the Florida Marlins and the Colorado Rockies. They did not play a game until 1993.

---

2   Sometimes called the "Senior Circuit" because it is 25 years older than the American League, which wasn't founded until 1901. This is the kind of thing you've been spared if you think the Rockies are a mountain range. Again, congratulations.

So when I tell you their legal eagles were in the arena battling in 1991, you know you have a precocious franchise on your hands.

The Rockies chose purple and black for their colors. They chose an interlocking CR as their cap logo and jersey decoration. Folks in Denver began buying caps and jerseys. Folks from as far away as Nebraska and the Dakotas identified with the team,[3] and Rockies gear was selling faster than snow blowers and ski poles.

Until the Rockies got a very nice letter from the legal department of a San Antonio dry ice company called Carbonic Reserves. Seems Carbonic Reserves had a logo. They didn't have team jerseys and hats, they didn't have a stadium or a scoreboard, but they had been using an interlocked CR on their stationery and their trucks and their ... I don't know, their dry ice buckets, I guess ... for many years. They had trademarked it.

Oops.

So you've been the lawyer for the Colorado Rockies for about an hour-and-a-half when the phone rings and they tell you the millions of dollars of team gear that's being sold infringes on someone else's trademark and you need to take care of it. Preferably before lunch.

This is not an auspicious start. Baseball players cost more than jumbo jets and break down more than Studebakers. If you're gonna have to stock a baseball team with the requisite number of multimillionaires to begin competition, you don't have a lot of disposable cash to throw around on legal fees.

One wag suggested the team settle by agreeing to refer to its bench-warmers as "the carbonic reserves."

But the Texans were not litigious.[4] I don't have access to the exact terms of the settlement, but it was considerably cheaper than a minor-league second baseman, did not require designating players "carbonic" anything, and left the Rockies enough money for bats, balls, cleats, and all the other stuff my dad hated buying.

---

3 So help me, they sold season tickets to people in North Dakota. That's 81 games a year, played 800 miles away. Apparently Mom had relatives in North Dakota she didn't tell me about.

4 There's a sentence you don't get to write often.

But a couple of decades down the road, the Rockies have run into more Intellectual Property trouble. The Carbonic Reserves case may have just been the opening salvo of a hitherto unknown curse.

Seems the team wanted to use Rockies.com for its website. Makes sense. We sports fans are easily confused. Having to type something as complicated as ColoradoRockies.com might be too much for us. Especially since it would require us to be able to spell Colorado, something that probably requires even a few Rockies *players* to look at the scoreboard

But someone – or something – else already had Rockies.com.

Canada.

More specifically, the Canadian Tourism Authority.

For the Canadian Rockies. The mountains.

So the phone rang in the legal-department bullpen. Again. And the Rockies' lawyers went to work.

They must be great negotiators. They got the website for only 1.2 million dollars.

One point two million. Dollars. American. To change from ColoradoRockies.com to just plain Rockies.com.

That may not sound like a bargain to you. GoDaddy.com charges a dollar a month, which means the Rockies could have purchased one of their domain names and been paid up until the year 102,013 for the same money.[5]

Or, for 1.2 million dollars, you could keep the old website and pay for an education campaign that would teach even the densest of us fans to spell Colorado. After all, most of us can already spell "color" so the ad campaign practically writes itself.

So what makes this such a great deal for the "Rox"?[6] Why am I so impressed with their legal department's negotiating skills? What

---

5 And I dare say GoDaddy.com would have given them a nice discount for paying 100,000 years in advance.

6 Apparently Denver headline writers don't even want to struggle through "Rockies." They typically shorten the team name and *never* attempt "Colorado."

makes this a settlement comparable to The Great Carbonic Reserves Swindle of '91?

They got Major League Baseball to pay for it.

That's right. Major League Baseball is an entity.[7] If you saw *The Exorcist* or any of the *Final Destination* movies you know what I'm talking about.[8]

And somehow the Rockies were able to convince them that getting a simple website for simple Colorado baseball fans was their responsibility. I was not privy to these negotiations, but I have to assume they involved signing over at least a *couple* of souls.

Seems MLB had bought Angels.com in 2010 for my favorite team, the Los Angeles Angels of Anaheim.[9] In 2010, MLB spent $200K for Angels.com.[10] In doing so, they set a precedent the Rockies' legal department doubtless paraded back and forth in front of them in full equitable regalia.

Uncle Jack Baseball caved. Baseball the Entity bowed to precedent and shelled out a million two.

So learn from the Colorado Rockies and MLB: before you enter into a settlement, consider how it will affect your business in the future. There are still four baseball teams whose natural websites belong to someone else.[11] And at the rate website costs are skyrocketing, MLB could end up having to give away the store for Rays.com or Rangers.com.[12]

---

7   Or, as the Supreme Court would put it, "a person." I like to think of it as "Uncle Jack."

8   And if you saw any of the *Final Destination* movies, you are in no position to look down your nose at my baseball habit.

9   And you do NOT want to get me started on THAT name.

10 I don't even want to think about who owned Angels.com. I'm just gonna assume it was a "higher authority" than the Canadian Tourism Board.

11 Twins.com belongs to a pair of brothers, Durland and Darvin Miller, who are doubtless licking their chops and pricing Bentleys right now. (Honest. It belongs to twins.)

12 But see, Darren Heitner, *Forbes Magazine*, Jan. 9, 2013, "Did MLB Overpay by Spending 1.2 Million for Rockies.com?"

Even my mom wouldn't spend that much. Although, in 1962, she did spend $15 we didn't have on the most beautiful Rawlings baseball glove I'd ever seen ... God rest her soul.

Primates in Pakistan

When my daughter Caitlin was a little girl, she watched me at the computer one day and then approached her mother. "Is Daddy mad?" she asked. Her mother answered, "I don't think so. Why?" "Because he's banging on the keyboard really hard," said the distressed 9-year-old.

Her mother had to explain to Caitlin that Daddy always banged on the keyboard. The "keyboards" Daddy learned to type on back in the Pleistocene *required* banging. They were much like Daddy's brain: unresponsive to finesse and programmed for a certain amount of resistance.

I've never refined my typing technique. You can tell from outside my office whether I'm at the keyboard. People unfamiliar with the sound back away from the door, expecting a herd of stampeded hamsters to come thundering out of chambers at any moment.

But I've elevated my game in other aspects of computer usage. I can track down cases on the Internet, buy Christmas presents without going to a mall, track down and watch bootleg videos of obscure musicians I like on my laptop.[1] I can read books, play scrabble[2], and identify obscure musicians I like[3] on my phone.

I'm never going to be able to *reside* in the electronic world of the 21st century, but I've gotten to the point I can walk through it without feeling like I'm liable to be mugged at any moment.

Which apparently differentiates me from the nation of Pakistan.

Pakistan decided a couple of months ago that it needed to control the Internet. Yeah, right. Them and King Canute.

Anyone who has raised even one child to the age of 15 knows you cannot control the Internet. It's the boogeyman, the Borg, the Creature from the Black Lagoon. It's the alien intelligence whose celestial arrival we've been dreading for decades. It just came from cyberspace rather than outer space.

Putting the Pakistanis up against it is like putting Bonzo the Chimp up against King Kong with a Glock.

Pakistan's opening salvo was censorship. They decided if they could just eliminate bad words from the Internet, it would be safe for their citizens' morals. So they announced that certain words and phrases would not be allowed.

I know what you're thinking. George Carlin's seven words you can't say on television, right?

Well, not exactly.

---

1   Listening to Greg Trooper doing "Muhammad Ali (The Meaning of Christmas)" or "They Call me Hank" would be worth the cost of the computer all by itself.

2   Yeah, I know Zynga calls it Words with Friends; I could call this column *War and Peace*, but it wouldn't turn it into Tolstoy. I'm old, not amnesiac. I know Scrabble when I see it.

3   And on the eighth day, God created the Shazam app.

How about 1,100 banned words and phrases?

That's right. Eleven hundred things you can't say on the Internet in Pakistan or they will come and pour orange juice onto your keyboard.[4]

It's an impressive list. Well, maybe not "impressive," exactly. What adjective would you use if you found out your next door neighbor collected road kill and had filled three bedrooms of his home with it – segregated according to whether it had fur, feather, or shell? That's what this list is like.

The list is largely an encyclopedic collection of sex terms demonstrating a mastery of lowlife sexual slang that reflects badly on the Pakistani censors. Hard to look at the words and phrases they thought of to ban without wondering how they got to know so many disgusting terms.

There are things you would expect on the list, like "damn" and "go to hell" and "quickie." Carlin's words are on the list.[5]

And there are things you might not have expected but don't really find surprising. I would put "flogging the dolphin" into this category. I'm not really sure what "flogging the dolphin" refers to, but I'm not prepared to defend any of the things – literal or figurative – that come immediately to mind, so I can't really say I'm offended by Pakistan putting it on the banned list.

And there are things that seem ... um ... counterintuitive, like "penthouse" and "hostage" and "looser." There are hundreds of words like these that just seem rather random. "Harder"? Really? "Deeper"? Better not discuss diamonds or swimming pools online.

And then there are the things that are just downright mystifying. You violate Pakistani law if you sit down in Islamabad and transmit the word "deposit." Honest. "Deposit" is on the list. On line banking will henceforth be conducted by standing in line at Pakistani banks.

---

4   Eleven hundred and nine, actually, but I thought I'd round it off just to show I knew how.

5   As are a host of words Carlin wouldn't have thought of if you'd given him a month and a lot of bad weed.

"Athlete's foot" is on the list. So don't go looking for podiatric help on the web. Your toes start itching, spray paraquat on them and hope for the best.

Both "sex" and "no sex" are on the list. So they've got you coming and going on that one.[6]

"Gonnorehea" is on the list. NO, not "gonnorhea." That didn't make the list. *Gonorrehea.* With an extra "e." If you can spell, you can discuss gonorrhea on the Internet in Pakistan. That's your reward for paying attention in sex ed class. Apparently – all indications to the contrary notwithstanding – the government values education.

The next word on the list after the rather embarrassing gonorrhea loophole was completely dumbfounding to me: gonzagas. I knew of only two meanings for "Gonzaga": a small Jesuit university in eastern Washington and the guy the small Jesuit university in eastern Washington was named after.

Now, the university in Washington has made a lot of enemies in the last decade by turning out a basketball team whose success has far outstripped anything a tiny school in the Palouse should be able to accomplish. If they had made the list of words banned at Indiana University or North Carolina or UCLA, I could understand it. But Pakistan?

Well . . . it turns out "gonzagas" has acquired a secondary meaning. Yeah, you won't have to work too hard on this one. Just note that the slang term is plural and ask yourself what plural thing my gender is most hung up on.

Yep. So no Pakistani scholarship kids at Gonzaga for the foreseeable future. And the next time I'm inclined to leer at a woman in a bikini, the image of one of the Jesuits who taught me in college will pop into my head.[7]

The one that really makes me feel old is "glazed donut." Apparently there is some sexual connotation to that phrase that I am too old to

---

6   And yes, one of the words in that sentence is on the list.

7   The Pakistanis missed a good bet, here. They should be *encouraging* the use of the term "gonzagas". Hard to imagine anything could discourage promiscuity more effectively than having images of Jesuits pop into your head when you look at women.

recognize. And what's worse, I've reached the age where there are days when a glazed doughnut might interest me more than sex.[8]

But the *pièce de résistance*, the absolute zenith of goofy censorial policy, is a phrase I absolutely cannot think of without laughing. The government of the sovereign state of Pakistan has declared it illegal to introduce into web commerce the phrase … wait for it … monkey crotch.

That's right. Monkey crotch.

If you juxtapose online the word "monkey" followed by the word "crotch" you have violated the laws of Pakistan. And while I don't know much about the Pakistani correctional system,[9] I'm pretty sure if you go to jail there behind a "monkey crotch" beef, you automatically become the [insert banned Pakistani Internet word here] of another inmate.

Let me digress for just a moment. Years ago, I received a letter months after it was mailed. Stamped on the front of it in purple ink were the words, "Found in supposedly empty equipment."

The letter was not important, and I could certainly see how a few of the trillions of letters mailed every year could get lost in "supposedly empty equipment." Anybody who's left a sock in the dryer understands that.

What bothered me was that this apparently happened so often the Post Office had a *stamp* for it. Rather than telling their people to be really careful when they took the socks out of the dryer, the Post Office had just prepared a stamp for every branch to use when this happened.

That's kinda what bothers me about the banning of "monkey crotch." It's not so much that they've banned it. I'm certainly not going to miss it. In my whole life, I have never felt the need to use the phrase

---

8   I did not look up glazed donut for a secondary meaning. I was afraid it would force me to give up something I am not prepared to do without.

9   I saw *Midnight Express* thirty years ago and it so terrified me I have made a point of not learning anything more about Middle Eastern prisons. At about the same time, I saw *Deliverance* and never got into another canoe.

"monkey crotch." In all the times I've been to the zoo or watched Wild Kingdom or torn my pants, I've never felt the need to utter that phrase.

But in Pakistan – *a nation that has nuclear bombs* – the construction "monkey crotch" apparently comes up often enough that the government felt the need to address its use in electronic media.

Monkey crotch.

That terrifies me. A nation that couldn't find Osama Bin Laden in their sock drawer has nuclear weapons and monkey-crotch issues. So be afraid. Be very afraid.

Lord help us all if they get a zoo.

Planes, Trains and . . . Cows

Legend has it that the publication of *The Great Gatsby* pushed Ernest Hemingway into a deep depression. Hemingway is supposed to have confided to friends that he found it difficult to write after reading *Gatsby* because it had been his dream to write The Great American Novel and Fitzgerald had beaten him to it. Now I know how he felt.

My dream was less Homeric than Hemingway's. I figured with my talent, I needed to set the bar lower. Setting it on the ground seemed appropriate, but I was afraid if the bar were lying in the dirt, others might have difficulty recognizing it as a bar and trip over it, exposing me and the state[1] to civil liability. So I set it about ankle high.

I set it not at the Great American Opinion, nor the Great Californian Opinion. I wasn't even going for the Great American Assumption of the Risk Opinion or the Greatest Single Issue Discussion of the Last Decade. Those all seemed way too high for my modest leaping ability.[2]

I set my sights on the perfect paragraph. That seemed high enough to keep people from tripping over and low enough to be doable. I figured I had twelve years before the electorate got wise to me and threw me out at the end of my term, and in that time I should be able to write one perfect paragraph.

I may have been right. I'm halfway through my term now and haven't done it yet, but I've written a few I liked that survived the Supreme Court's scythe. It may be that another six years of honing my skills might have resulted in one perfect paragraph. But I'm afraid my heart's not in it anymore.

The Court of Appeals for the Eleventh Appellate District, in Portage County, Ohio, did it a few months ago. And now anything I wrote would be a pale imitation of their *Gatsby* paragraph.

Say what you will about me, I know when I'm beat. Here is the first paragraph of *Mayor v. Wedding*, 2003 WL 22931354 (Ohio App. 11 Dist.): "In this case we are called on to determine whether a cow is an uninsured motor vehicle under appellants' insurance policy. We hold that it is not."

How could you improve on that? I mean, that's "Call me Ishmael." That's "All happy families are happy alike, all unhappy families are

---

1   Yeah, I know it's supposed to be "the state and me," but that misstates the relative importance of the parties. Sometimes grammar has to take a backseat to accuracy.

2   Besides, as Tom Crosby used to say, "All my best stuff gets reversed."

unhappy in their own way." That's "It was a dark and stormy night . . ."[3] No one could read that paragraph and stop. It is, therefore, not only the perfect paragraph, but also the perfect *opening* paragraph. My desolation is complete.

Oh, sure, you could quibble about the "that" in the second sentence. It serves no obvious purpose, and slows down the sentence. But, then again, maybe you *want* to slow down the sentence at that point. Content this rare should be savored, and slowing the reader down there may provide an extra moment to luxuriate in the richness of two sentences of such magnificent lunacy. Maybe that "that" makes it the *pluperfect* paragraph.

It's truly inspiring to see colleagues rise to the level of their material. I mean, when you get a case which actually requires you to decide whether a cow is a motor vehicle, it deserves some beautiful writing, and this court – most notably Judge Cynthia Westcott Rice, who authored the opinion – provided it, right from the overture.

Why don't I get cases like that – I mean why besides the fact we have more left-handed Nepalese Communists than cows wandering the roads of Orange County.

That's how this came up. The Mayors were driving along Interstate 76 one evening when their car struck a cow owned by Mr. Wedding. Since Mr. Wedding and his cow were uninsured for this eventuality, the Mayors sued their own automobile insurance carrier, contending they should receive compensation under the uninsured motorist provision of their policy.[4] The insurer, predictably hypertechnical and mendacious, fell back on the picayune cavil that in order to have a motorist

---

3   There is absolutely nothing wrong with, "It was a dark and stormy night." What got E. G. Bulwer-Lytton in trouble wasn't the part of the line Snoopy always emulated, but the rest of it. The full quote is, "It was a dark and stormy night; the rain fell in torrents – except at occasional intervals, when it was checked by a violent gust of wind which swept up the streets (for it is in London that our scene lies), rattling along the housetops, and fiercely agitating the scanty flame of the lamps that struggled against the darkness." Now *that's* a sentence in serious need of a compass.

4   Timothy A. Ita of Cleveland, Ohio, was able to make this argument to an appellate court with a straight face. Remind me never to play poker with Mr. Ita.

– insured or uninsured – you need a motor vehicle, and that the cow did not qualify.

Apparently, large farm animals in the road are a recurring problem in Ohio. In deciding this case, the court was able to refer to not just one, but *two* precedents in which motorists had tried similar arguments. Wow. You give me that kind of run support, I could throw a few shut-outs myself.

Honest. Two precedents. In 1984, the Ohio appellate courts decided *State Automobile Mutual Insurance Co. v. Cleveland Carriage Co.*, 98 Ohio App. 3d 361, which, according to the *Mayor* court – and I have no reason to doubt them – held that a horse was not a motor vehicle.

Then, extending that ruling to hitherto unimagined lengths, they decided in 1991 that attaching a buggy to the horse did not turn either the horse or the buggy into a MOTOR vehicle. (*Wilbur v. Allstate Ins. Co.*, 11th Dist. No. 90-G-1000, 1991 WL 252851). Ohio is obviously a tough place to be livestock, but apparently Shangri-La for appellate counsel.

So how, you might ask, did the courts in Ohio come to the conclusion that neither a horse nor a cow is a MOTOR vehicle? How, you might wonder, did they sift through all the legal chaff to find the kernel of logic that separates warm-blooded barnyard animals from lifeless, steel MOTOR vehicles?

Go ahead, ask. Wonder.

Was it by taking judicial notice of the conspicuous absence of MOTORS in cows and horses? No, no. That would be way too easy. Nobody remembers opinions like that. No one writes odes to such pro-saic analysis. Who would remember Mays' catch in the '54 World Series if he'd turned at the last moment and caught it facing home plate?

No, the 11th District went for the three-cushion, double-kiss into the side pocket, using a bridge to make the shot. Their analysis (drum roll, please):

There appears to be no dispute that there was a collision; the cow was not insured at the time of the collision; and that the cow caused the collision. The dispute in this case is whether the cow was a "land motor vehicle" as defined in the policy. While a cow is designed for operation on land, we do not believe a cow is a "motor vehicle." The policy at issue does not separately define "motor vehicle;" therefore we must look to the common, ordinary meaning of this term.

The American Heritage Dictionary defines "motor vehicle" as, "a self-propelled, wheeled conveyance that does not run on rails." Id. at 817, 374 N.E.2d 146. A cow is self-propelled, does not run on rails, and could be used as a conveyance; however, there is no indication in the record that this particular cow had wheels. Therefore, it was not a motor vehicle and thus was not a "land motor vehicle" as defined in the policy. The trial court properly found that appellants were not entitled to uninsured motorist coverage. [Citations to the two precedents noted above.]

That's right. The reasoning process wasn't that you can't be a motor vehicle if you don't have a motor. It was that YOU CAN'T BE A MOTOR VEHICLE IF YOU DON'T HAVE WHEELS!

Lord help the people of Ohio if their legislature ever passes laws pertaining to "wheeled vehicles." The whole state appellate system will herniate trying to figure out how to define "wheeled vehicles" now that they've already defined "motor vehicles" as vehicles with wheels.

Actually, I never met these people, but my instinct is that Judge Rice and her concurring colleagues, William M. O'Neill and Diane V. Grendell, are having more fun than any of us west of the Taft family ever suspected. And I don't for a moment begrudge them that fun. In fact, if I could get me, Corrigan and Gomes – or me, Parilli and Manoukian, or even me and any two people who drink too much – transferred to the same division, we could probably come up with some pretty fancy ways to differentiate cows from automobiles or ducks from tangerines or sheep from shinola. We might even find a way to match *Mayor v. Wedding.*

But I know we couldn't top it. Because I know that, confronted with the same case, I would have failed to rise to the material. I know I would not have produced the perfect paragraph.

My opinion would have recited the facts in a single paragraph and then held, "Hello? It's a cow."

That kind of work does not get you the office next to the Chief Justice.

But, then again, I still have six years left.

SEND IN THE CLOWNS

There were no lawyers in my family, so lawyer jokes were considered fair game. To the rest of the world, lawyers are the perfect game animals: big, slow afoot, and tasty. My family was no exception.

And since my roots are in the South, most of the jokes involved southern lawyers. One I loved as a boy involved a criminal defense attorney explaining to the jury in closing argument why they should acquit his client of theft:

"Y'all have watched my client here in court for five days. He is not an attractive man. Hell's fire, let's be honest, folks, he's ugly as sin."

"And y'all heard him testify. You know he's not the sharpest tool in the shed. Having worked with him for several weeks now, I can attest to the fact he has the personality of an elm stump and the IQ of a lemon meringue pie. Boy's dumb as a bag o' hammers."

"So I ask you now to consider those facts in light of your own experience and your knowledge that our God is both all-powerful and all-merciful. And I know if you do that, you will have to acquit. I mean, think about it, folks, would an all-powerful and all-merciful God make a man ugly and stupid AND a thief?"

Now THAT'S a closing argument.

I've taken comfort from that story over the years when I thought I understood something and judges or attorneys insisted I was wrong. I would simply remind myself that an all-powerful and all-merciful God would not have made me unattractive, unhealthy, AND stupid.

Now we might argue over the logic of that statement.[1] Indeed, if you practice in Orange County you may already have had occasion to argue my logic with me ... in court. But the major and minor premises of the syllogism are pretty solid – especially the unhealthful one.

So far, I have had a tonsillectomy, an appendectomy, subacute bacterial endocarditis I and II, facial paralysis I, II, and III, multiple kidney stones, several dislocated joints, a lifetime of migraines, asthma, knee surgery, hip replacement surgery, two oral surgeries, kidney surgery, brain surgery, and heart surgery. This is, truth be told, your basic bad body.

So I know my way around a doctor's office. And the fact these people have kept me shiny side up through all these travails has made me a big fan of the medical profession. I am loath to second-guess them when it comes to medical judgment.

Which makes it all the more surprising to me that they are so anxious to practice law. Every time I go in there, they hand me contracts that require me to waive most of my constitutional rights, all of my free will, and at least three guarantees of the Magna Carta.

---

1   Actually, "logic" kind of overstates the case; it's more like intellectual comfort food.

"The doctor will see you as soon as you sign this." And, of course, signing it requires me to agree to arbitration.

I used to fight this. I am, of course, part of the very system they want me to opt out of. I believe in that system. Asking me to agree to arbitration is like asking a Roman Catholic cardinal to agree that his afterlife will be decided by a panel of Lutherans.

So I used to refuse to sign the form, and the receptionist would look at me like I had walked in with dynamite strapped to my chest and a detonator in my hand.

She would send me back to see the doctor, who would sit down with me and explain that his lawyer drew up this form – often a lawyer I knew – and that he would treat me without it if I insisted but he would really appreciate it if I would sign it.

And I, to my utter amazement, would be so charmed and beguiled by how reasonable he was being, so anxious to be as nice as he was, that I would sign it and give up my right to jury trial, my right to counsel, my Eighth Amendment rights, my *Faretta* rights, the mineral rights to my back yard, and my first born.

I was so easy.

After awhile, I just stopped reading them. Like most people, I want fast treatment more than I want a good forum for my complaints, so I now skim the form and sign it. Someday an unscrupulous dentist will probably hold a quitclaim on my house.

My wife, on the other hand, approaches arbitration agreements the same way she approaches snakes she comes across hiking in the canyons: she is determined only one of them will come out alive and utterly convinced her bite is worse than theirs.

Kelly takes no prisoners. She not only refuses to arbitrate, she demands a jury trial before a panel of plaintiffs' attorneys and people rejected by medical schools. She crosses out provisions in the form, writes in her own, adds codicils and appendices, and pretty much agrees to nothing other than her willingness to stop suing when the doctor proves he is out of money and has no solvent living relatives.

When it comes to arbitration agreements, Kelly is not so much an attorney as a flame-thrower.

So when she went in for her yearly mammogram last week, it figured to be the worst mismatch ever that did not involve anyone named Reno or Benteen.

Sure enough, they had stuff they wanted her to sign. But this time, she couldn't just write all over it because it was electronic. They had her sit at a desk with a little screen and asked her to sign the "agreement" on the screen. Kelly girded her loins[2] and started in on what the screen entitled "Condition of Admission."

The first thing she noted was that it was a *singular* "condition" rather than *plural* "conditions." That would have been encouraging except for the fact the first heading "Physicians are Independent Contractors" was numbered "7." One of the things Kelly has learned in 25 years of practice is to distrust documents that BEGIN with "7." Not only was there obviously more than one "Condition of Admission," but most of them were either invisible or hiding.

This did not augur well. But my wife is a reasonable woman. She was willing to give these people a chance. She read and initialed Provision 7.

But Provision 8, entitled "Acknowledgements," said, "This is to acknowledge that the undersigned has been given the Notice of Privacy Practice, Important Patient Information, Patient's Rights and Responsibilities and patient Safety Statement." So Kelly asked for them.

The receptionist looked at her like she had suddenly begun speaking in tongues. "Those are just acknowledgements," the receptionist said. "They just mean you acknowledge the conditions under which you're being treated."

"And what are those?" Kelly asked. "What are the conditions?"

The receptionist now realized she had a troublemaker on her hands. This woman actually wanted to KNOW the conditions under which she was being treated, before agreeing to them. Danged harpy.

---

2   I have no idea what that means, but it sounded vaguely sexy, and I thought it might spice up the story.

The receptionist left and returned with a sheaf of papers. Anyone who has practiced civil litigation – and Kelly has – knows this technique: bury them in discovery.

Kelly was not at all intimidated. She pulled out her red pen and began marking them up. By the time she was halfway through, the "Condition of Admission" – all four pages of it – looked like the battlefield at Antietam.

Kelly was writing "I do not agree," and crossing things out, and just generally lopping off clauses like she was Innocent I, going through and weeding out unacceptable gospels to arrive at today's Bible.

She was, however, a little nonplussed when she came to a provision that required her to agree to the release of information and provided, "If the patient[3] or the patient's legal representative[4] does not want such information to be released, he/she may check the box indicated below." There was no box.

Kelly pointed this out to the receptionist. Her response was, "Oh, we would never disclose any information about you unless you agreed."

"But that's exactly what it says you will do unless I check the nonexistent box," Kelly protested. Kelly's not sure, but she thinks this is when the receptionist suggested she might be in the wrong office and asked if she was looking for psychiatric care.

Which would have explained the "Consent to Photograph" provision.

That provision provided, "During hospitalization, the patient may be visited by celebrities, clowns, musicians, or other entertainers." It went on to require, as a "condition of admission" that Kelly agree to being photographed with these people. Honest.

Really? Clowns? She came in for a mammogram and they were refusing to do it unless she agreed to be photographed with clowns?

That's what it said. It said, "The pictures may be used in newspapers, magazines, on television, or in hospital publications."

---

3   That would be Kelly.

4   That would be Kelly.

I've never had a mammogram.[5] Kelly tells me they're unpleasant, and I can understand – and even fully support – efforts to make them more enjoyable.

Musicians... entertainers? Maybe a good idea. Cutting edge medicine.

But clowns? In the middle of a discussion about legal rights and forums the hospital inserts a clause about clown photos? That just seemed so random and bizarre that Kelly not only wrote in Antietam red ink her refusal to agree to it but also questioned it to the supervisor with whom she was now dealing.[6]

That's when it began to dawn on them that maybe this was not a problem patient. Maybe these were problem documents.

Sure enough. Seems the little hospital in our town was recently swallowed – or rescued[7] – by a much bigger hospital. The bigger hospital is a chain which includes a children's hospital. When they took over the smaller hospital, they wanted to use their own forms, but mistakenly sent over some from the children's hospital.

Clowns and ballplayers and celebrities often show up at children's hospitals, and their visits are photographed. Not so much at mammograms, it turns out.[8] The hospital figured out the mistake and gave Kelly a different set of forms.[9]

So if you're going in for a mammogram in the near future, you can rest easy: you will not be required to pose for photos with clowns. My wife has slain that dragon for you.

As the old southern lawyer would have put it, no one should be required to submit to a mammogram, wear a hospital gown, AND be photographed with clowns.

---

5   I'm reaching that age where members of my gender start developing mammos, but my insurance company – doubtless run by men – has not yet required me to have them grammed.

6   By the time she refused to sign the clown codicil, Kelly was two levels of supervision above the receptionist. One more problem and they were going to turn her over to their leg-breaker.

7   In business, as in life, the distinction can sometimes be a fine one. Ask Jonah.

8   Which is probably just as well.

9   The children's hospital forms had been used for months – apparently without incident, thus confirming Kelly's belief she is the only person left on the planet that reads these things.

CARPENTRY WITHOUT TOOLS

My father was a casketmaker. He taught me not to judge the carpenter if you don't know his tools.

It was just a homey tradesman's adjuration not to be judgmental, and I remember as a boy being unimpressed by it as a mantra. But I sure appreciate it now. It has helped keep my blood pressure in check for many years.

I think of it often when I encounter an opinion I do not think is the author or panel's best work. I remind myself that I don't know how good the briefing was, I don't know what the record was like, and

– perhaps most important – I haven't sat down and struggled with the cases cited.

Every lawyer has had the experience of thinking he or she knew what a case said and then going back and finding the wording was *slightly* different than we remembered. And sometimes those slight differences can be crucial. So when I find that my colleagues have arrived at an opinion that is ... well, let's say counterintuitive ... I try to remember my dad, urging me not to judge the carpenter.

But Dad didn't say anything about carpenters who disdain tools and choose to work without them. I dunno, I think Dad would have made an exception for judging somebody who turned his back on chisel and plane and just beat on the wood with a rock.

So I'm not sure what to make of Justice Clarence Thomas' nine years of silence. Justice Thomas has not asked a question from the bench of the United States Supreme Court since February 22, 2006. We're approaching a decade of never needing enlightenment, clarification, or even a glass of water. That makes Pete Rose's streak look like child's play.[1]

The guy is deciding the most important and difficult questions in all of American jurisprudence. He's untangling knots lesser lights like myself didn't even know had been tied. He's wending his way through labyrinthine arguments so complex I could barely diagram the sentences, much less select the right legal path. And through all that, he has never felt the need to ask a single question?

I'll leave it up to you whether that is a reflection of true brilliance or a badge of arrogant lunacy. All I gotta say is he better be using magic hammers and enchanted nails, or even my dad would have to question his technique.

Oral argument is a critical part of appellate advocacy. If you're an appellate judge, do not read the rest of this paragraph because the next sentence will ruin your lunch. Here it is: I think no one should ever waive oral argument without a really good reason.

---

1   And we all know what happened to Rose.

Really good reasons might include:

1. my client can't afford it;

2. I am the worst public speaker since Chewbacca the Wookie;

3. there is a hole in my position big enough to drive a Peterbilt through and I don't want to be in front of it when they do;

4. my position is so clearly a winner that even *this* court can't botch it.

If you can't finish the sentence "I waived oral argument because ..." with something at least as convincing as those four clauses, don't do it. Find another analogy that fits your case or a new way of making the arguments you raised in your brief,[2] suit up, and go to court ready to help out.

I get a lot of help from good oral arguments. And as some of you know,[3] I need all the help I can get.

So unlike Justice Thomas, I ask a lot of questions. These generally break down into five categories.

The first reason I ask questions is that I really don't understand something counsel has said in the brief. I am clearly light years slower than Justice Thomas because there are often things I don't understand.

I find oral argument is a good place to clarify these things, at least now that the Commission on Judicial Performance has explained to me that calling appellant's counsel at home at 3 a.m. is not considered appropriate behavior.

They also didn't like me throwing pebbles against the window of counsel's condo and asking him to come down and explain pages 26 to

---

2 Don't try finding a new way to raise a *new* argument unless you own stock in an asbestos mine and have new products to try out because the court's response will be the appellate equivalent of Greek fire.

3 And the rest suspect.

31 of his brief to me. Maybe if I had federal marshals I could send out to interrogate counsel, I wouldn't need to ask questions at oral argument, but I don't, so I do.

Closely related to the "I'm afraid I don't understand this" question is the "I'm afraid I DO understand this" question. This exchange usually goes something like this:

"Mr. Roberts,[4] your argument, as I understand it, is that the evidence was insufficient to establish your client's membership in the street gang because he is from Uzbekistan. If I read your brief correctly, you conducted an exhaustive computer search of all California cases ever decided (including worker's comp and bankruptcy cases – which I thought showed admirable thoroughness), and there has never previously, in the entire history of California, been a street gang member of Uzbek descent. Is that correct?"

"Yes, your Honor, not a single one."[5]

"Alright ... um ... well, the Attorney General suggested in his respondent's brief that we should not only reject this argument but also publish the decision, so no one would ever be stupid enough to make that argument again. And while I feel that's a little harsh, I must say it's important to note that I only think it's a LITTLE harsh. Do you want to take another crack at expressing this point so as to maybe phrase it in such a way that you have a snowball's chance in hell of picking up my vote?"

The third category is the "Oh, come now" question. When I was an appellate lawyer, I used to insist that some day I would get up the nerve to respond to an opponent's brief with one that set out the facts, set out the issue raised by my opponent, and then, under "Discussion," said simply, "Oh, come now."

---

4   I'll ascribe this argument to Cliff Roberts. He didn't actually make it. Cliff has never, to my knowledge, made a bad argument in his life, but he has taken the position that since we're such great friends, he should be in the book. I don't have any friends better than Cliff, so I promised him I'd put him in the book. Here you are, Cliff.

5   Cliff's smile is now bright enough to make the electric lighting in the courtroom superfluous. He's hugely proud of this argument.

I never did it, so perhaps I wasn't as cocky as I was accused of being, but every now and again, someone will say something in court that is so outrageous, I can't ignore it. I don't actually say, "Oh, come now," but I think that thought might creep into my tone of voice when I ask the question.

These questions are almost always involuntary. That's why it amazes me that Justice Thomas hasn't even slipped into an "Oh, come now" question in four years.

I mean, I can be sitting there, absolutely determined that there is nothing this attorney can possibly say that will make me open my mouth. I've read the brief, I know his position, and I am thoroughly convinced by the brief that there is nothing he can say that is going to make the case easier for me to decide, so there is no reason to ask him a question. And then he will say, "Glockenspiels were grown hydroponically by the ancient Egyptians to enable them to ward off scurvy on their twice-monthly trips to West Palm Beach" – or the legal equivalent thereof – and I just can't help myself.

"Mr. Roberts," I'll say, "This is a new courtroom and we're still getting used to the acoustics. Could you please repeat what you just said? Because it *sounded* like you were talking about hydroponic glockenspiels, and I know that can't be the case."

How is it that Justice Thomas has not once blurted out an "Oh, come now" question? I mean, I know he doesn't have Cliff Roberts[6] appearing in front of him, but my own reading of Supreme Court jurisprudence convinces me lots of goofy things must get said there. How is it Justice Thomas has never challenged any of them?

How is it he hasn't thrown any batting practice fastballs up to the plate? This is my fourth category of appellate questions. It's something appellate justices do all the time.

It goes like this: You know there's at least one vote on the panel contrary to yours. So during argument you throw the side you're on a nice, soft 80 mph fastball to hit, a question so easy you expect them to

---

6   You're all over this one, Cliff.

whack it out of the park and help convince your contrarian colleague of the error of her ways.

This can be frustrating because attorneys asked questions at oral argument invariably assume the question is unfriendly. Even if it sounds easy, they wonder if there's a pit they're about to fall into. A friendly question is often so disconcerting they're confused by it and bungle the answer. In the parlance of our court, they foul it off.

We tease Justice Fybel about being the worst batting practice pitcher in the history of appellate law. God bless him, he's a brilliant jurist and a perennial nominee for World's Nicest Man, but every time he tosses up a soft one, counsel pops it into the seats behind home plate.

Why Justice Thomas doesn't use this device, I don't know. Maybe he was once hit by a foul ball.

He says he employs no questions because he already knows how he's going to vote, but that's not really the issue, is it? The issue is how the *court's* going to vote, and I can't understand passing on the chance to affect that by steering counsel in a direction you think might affect how *other* members of the court will vote.

I would have thought he would at least have employed a pity question once in the last four years. That's Category Five.

No one goes to the Supreme Court to argue alone. They all take their mom and dad and their spouse and kids and their sixth-grade teacher and their Little League coach to share the moment. You would think that after one of these poor souls has been publicly eviscerated in front of most of his family and the entire Chamber of Commerce of his home town, someone might ask him an easy question to allow him to get out of Dodge without bleeding to death right there in the courtroom.

I do that. I try to have a nice comment or an easy question for the guy who brought his client with him or the woman whose law school advocacy class is sitting behind her. If they take a beating,[7] I try really hard to find some verbal analgesic to spread on the wounds.

But not Justice Thomas. Nine years and no questions.

Hey, he's on the Supreme For Crying Out Loud Court. As the old adage goes, "They may not always be right, but they're always the Supreme Court." So if he asks no questions, it is *de facto*[8] the right way to go.

I only wish we could get Cliff Roberts in front of him. Then we'd see just how tight-lipped he really is.

---

7   And let's face it, we've all been there. The casketmaker aphorism for this experience is, "Ya gotta play the cards you're dealt." And when you play those cards at a table where there are three, seven, or nine other players and they're wearing black robes and you aren't, your pair of treys can put a serious hurt on you.

8   And when you're dealing with the Supreme Court, the difference between *de facto* and *de jure* is pretty much academic.

NUCKIN FUTS

Intellectual property law is not my long suit. In fact, you may have heard it suggested that I might be a little short-suited on intellectual property itself.

So I can't say I was real excited when my son told me there was an Australian intellectual property case I just *had to read*. Really? Australian intellectual property law? A must read?

I have enough trouble keeping up with American law.[1] I try not to publish much because I figure the more cases I publish the more law there is to learn.

So branching out into antipodean law just seemed like walking into a biker bar in a Savile Row suit. "Hey, Dad, here's some more stuff that you can be baffled by," was not the kind of invitation designed to set my heart atingle.[2]

But I may have misjudged this one ... so to speak. The Aussie case presents a problem I've never seen before, and my response to it kinda surprises me. I may actually be siding with the grownups on this one.

I don't usually do that. I'm not yet a You-kids-get-offa-my-lawn kinda guy. I'm still a lot more likely to suggest people "lighten up" or "chill" than I am to shout, "Turn down that music!" I'm still surprised when I realize I'm not the target audience of the Jack-in-the-Box and Carl's Jr. commercials.

So I was a little taken aback when I found myself thinking the Australian government should have taken a stricter position against free speech in this case. It was kinda like hearing myself complain that a movie had too many scantily clad young women in it.

Here's the deal. An Australian snack food company applied for permission to market their product as "Nuckin Futs." They were rejected. As explained by the *Melbourne Herald Sun*, "The Trade Marks Examiner ruled that Nuckin Futs was an 'obvious spoonerism' and deemed it ineligible for registration under section 42 of the Trade Marks Act." In short, they decided the name was crass and indecent, and should not assault the eyes or vibrate against the eardrums of Australians.

I had no strong reaction to that decision, one way or the other.

I will admit to being a little tone-deaf on the issue of profanity. My mother grew up with Emily Post, place settings that included two forks and two spoons, and men who moderated their speech in the presence

---

1   Another thing you might have heard suggested.

2   I figure if I can get away with antipodean, I can get away with atingle.

of women. But Dad was a marine paratrooper whose first high school graduation was mine.

He had worked in the fields as a boy, voted dead people's names for Harry Truman's minions while still in grade school, and spent more time in the brig than on the parade ground. By the time he met Mom, his vocabulary was pretty fully formed ... and pretty full.

Mom did what she could, and Dad, to his credit, cleaned up his act pretty well. But profanity was still a natural part of my boyhood home and the blue-collar neighborhood in which I lived. I've never been especially uncomfortable with it, and my personal thesaurus includes a lot of words Mom would not have approved.

So I wasn't offended by the snack food company's product name, but neither was I throwing rocks at the Trade Marks Examiner for refusing to allow it. While I probably wouldn't have gone so far as to call it "scandalous" and "offensive" – as he did – I couldn't really get worked up about his decision.

Seemed like dog-bites-man news. Hardly seemed like news at all, in fact.

So imagine my amazement when the Trade Marks Examiner *reversed* himself.

That's right. Aussie solicitor named Jamie White appealed the ruling on the basis that " 'Nuckin Futs' is not offensive because it is commonplace in everyday Australian language." He contended the words "f..." and 'f...ing" were "now part of the universal discourse of the ordinary Australian."

And the Australian government bought it. After a year-long appellate process, they decided ... well, I don't know, apparently they decided that Australians were crass and indecent and the mark rather suited them. It was registered in April.

The only restriction is that the snack food folks had to agree not to market their product to children. So the futs folk have assured the

Australian government that the nuts will be sold only in pubs, night-clubs, and "other entertainment venues."[3]

So if you go to Australia– and visit a pub or nightclub[4] – you can buy Nuckin Futs.

To go with your Buckin Feer.

I have never been to Australia. But, as I am myself a descendant of deportees, I have always felt a kinship with them. And they invented Australian Rules Football,[5] which convinces me they share my affection for absolute lunacy. They seem like my kind of people.

But I wonder if they haven't gone a little far in coarsening the public discourse this way. I mean, can't you just hear the pub-goers next month, "Hey, Mate, bring me some Nuckin Futs while we watch the Uckin Folympics on the tuckin felly."

This is gonna get *way* out of hand.

And the whole idea you can keep this away from the children by requiring the product to be marketed in adult venues seems uncharac-teristically naive. There's a place for the delightful Australian optimism that is such a big part of their great national charm, but I don't think this is it.

You just know the little nippers[6] are gonna tumble to this pretty quickly. Hell,[7] this is an idea guaranteed to appeal more to the kids than it does to the adults. Grown-up Australians may well choose their snack foods based on taste and price, but no 12-year-old is going to pass up a chance to order Nuckin Futs even if they cost five bucks and taste like Duckin Firt.

And I'm a little disappointed that the Australian government has essentially thrown in the towel on the fight against vulgarity. Really,

---

3   Apparently, you're not supposed to use the phrase "strip joint" in a trademark application. Australia does have *some* standards.

4   I know you would never frequent a strip joint.

5   In case you thought maybe the Belgians had invented Australian Rules Football.

6   Pretty sure they have nippers in Australia.

7   Sorry, Mom.

Australia? That word has become part of the "universal discourse of Australians"? Really? *Universal?*

Not my call, of course. Given the actions of my own government of late, I'm really not in a position to question someone else's. And since I sometimes use the adjectival form of that word myself, I'm living in a Huckin Glass Fouse, here. So I won't be casting any stones.

But somehow I expect major world governments to exercise more restraint than I do. Dang,[8] what good is a government if its standards aren't higher than mine?

So I would have gotten this one wrong. I would have turned down the trademark. I would've yelled at the snack food people to get off my lawn and to take their Nuckin Futs with them.

And – apparently – Australia would have told me to chill.

Muckin Afazing.

---

8 I'm tryin', Mom; I'm *really* tryin'.

Voodoo Economics

Some say the world will end in fire,
Some say in ice.
From what I've tasted of desire
I hold with those who favor fire.

Me, I hold with those who favor numbers.

I think the world is going to end in some kind of apocalyptic numerical conflagration that will make the Big Bang look like stepped-on bubble wrap.

I have no idea how this is going to happen, any more than Robert Frost did when he wrote *Fire and Ice*. But I am thoroughly convinced our dependence on numbers exceeds our ability to comprehend them, and that it's going to turn around someday and bite us in ... well, not to put too fine a point on it ... the ass.

Zeroes are the big problem. We're drowning in zeroes. We're confronted every day with numbers so huge that we've lost our ability to comprehend their enormousness.[1]

Remember the joke going around at the end of the last administration? An aide runs into President Bush's office and says, "Mr. President, I have bad news: 15 Brazilian soldiers from our international peacekeeping force in Afghanistan have been killed in an ambush." To which the President replies, "That's terrible. Horrible. But tell me, son, just how many is a Brazilian?"

That's what we've come to. The numbers we're struggling with are so big we aren't even able to recognize their names anymore.

Ev Dirksen's sixties' vintage joke that, "A billion dollars here, a billion dollars there, pretty soon you're talking about real money," is no longer a joke; it's become reality. We're talking about spending a billion dollars the way we used to talk about re-paving a section of road.

We just can't comprehend billions and trillions. Hell, judging by the contracts we're handing out to second basemen and rock bass men, the concept of a mere *million* dollars seems to exceed our ability to cerebrate.

For the last decade, large-company CEO's have been getting eight-figure bonuses. EIGHT FIGURES. As in, "Thank you for running our company this year, here's $40,000,000 to go with your salary and stock options."

Come on, folks. Nobody's worth that kind of money. Nobody.

---

1   And allow me to indulge one of my pet peeves here. "Enormity" is not the noun form of "enormous." An enormity is a wicked or outrageous moral evil. "Enormity" does not convey size, it conveys depravity. Please don't file any more briefs complaining of the "enormity of the award" – at least not without recognizing the hyperbole involved in such a complaint.

The only reason they've been getting it is that the Boards of Directors of those companies – made up entirely of people who hope one day to BE the CEO and get the same stupidly excessive salary – agree to give it to them, and the stockholders are unable to comprehend just how much that is.

And please don't tell me the company needs to spend that much to get someone capable of running it. That's just silly. There are plenty of very capable people who would do it for a small fraction of that amount and – judging from the fiscal inanities of the last few years – do it just as well.[2]

Nor am I convinced by the lame-o argument that "the market" dictates such salaries, so they must be right. The whole concept of an omniscient market is that people will make rational choices in their own self-interest. The collective impact of those rational, self-interest-driven decisions will dictate supply and demand and keep the market from going seriously astray.

Which would be fine if people actually made rational decisions based on their own self-interest. They don't. They make stupid, self-destructive decisions every day.

Ask any realtor or automobile salesman about whether people make rational decisions based on their own self-interest *in making the biggest investments of their lives.* Ask the National Institute of Health if people make rational decisions based on their own self-interest on matters that will extend or shorten their lifespans.

Ask a family lawyer how people do in making rational decisions in their own self-interest about their families and loved ones – decisions that will determine how much they enjoy every waking moment.

Then talk to me about rational decisions based on self-interest.

You want proof? The people of the state of California, 4,206,284 of them, chose Arnold Schwarzenegger to be their governor. That was macro-self-destructive and pretty clearly irrational.

---

2   I, for example, would have driven Lehman Brothers off the cliff for a paltry $5 million. Less if I got good dental.

Arnold Schwarzenegger fathered a child by his maid. That was micro-self-destructive and cosmically irrational.

People make bad decisions like that all the time. The whole discipline of marketing and the entire industry of advertising are based in large measure on the self-evident fact that given the right encouragement, people will make bad decisions that are contrary to their self interest.

We all know that. And we know it's not just *other* people who make such decisions. We make them ourselves.

I will buy baked goods tomorrow. I have all my life. All I need to do is look in a mirror to realize this is not promoting my own self-interest.

But tomorrow, I will buy an apple fritter. Count on it.

If you can. It appears to me we've lost our basic ability to count. Either that or all those danged zeroes have clouded our minds to the point where we can't comprehend the significance of the counting.

The big news in May was that California miraculously found 6.6 BILLION DOLLARS it didn't know it had. Great news for the budget wonks; not so great – and damned scary – for those of us who want to believe the switchman hasn't fallen asleep.

Seems the expert economists relied upon by the state to predict its revenues had under-predicted by 6.6 billion dollars. That's 6,600,000,000. That's eight zeroes.

To help put that into perspective, the average California police officer makes $52,000 a year. For 6.6 billion dollars, we could pick 126, 923 of our poorest citizens, make them police officers, solve both the crime problem and the poverty problem, and have enough money left over for some apple fritters.

That's how much the "experts" missed by. Eight zeroes.

How did they make such a big mistake? Well, the only explanation I've heard was provided by an expert on NPR.[3]

He explained – so help me, I'm not making this up – that California has "a disproportionately high percentage of rich people."

---

3   I didn't catch his name, but he was on NPR, so he not only has to be an expert, he has to be an egghead.

I used to feel that way myself. Until I became a rich person. Now the number of rich people in California seems about right to me.[4]

The NPR guy explained that rich people rely not so much on salaries as on investment income.[5] And because they are rich, we never know what they're going to do with that income.

In this case, they seem to have chosen to realize the income, so we've been able to tax them on that realization, and – presto change-o, abracadabra – we ended up with an unexpected cement truck full of hundreds.

In other words, we looked behind the couch cushions after Justin Timberlake and Barry Bonds dropped by, and there it was: $6,600,000,000.

Voodoo economics has become a redundancy.

And it's affecting our judicial system. I heard a lawyer a few weeks ago lamenting the fact he was being "dragged back into court time after time over a $30,000 fee award."

The implication was clear: he couldn't believe anyone was expending so much effort over such a trifling amount.

I'm sorry. Thirty thousand dollars is – to borrow from Ev Dirksen – real money to me, and I think it should be to our profession.

I've been blessed both to have grown up blue-collar and to have worked with and before generations of lawyers and judges who appreciated zeroes. Men and women who had been through a Great Depression and a war that required rationing took decimal points seriously and they taught me to.

I got hit with a three-thousand-dollar dental bill last week and I'll probably be in a blue funk about it until the Cal-Fresno State

---

4   And make no mistake, I AM a rich person. I make over $200,000 a year. My father was a casket-maker. I know the difference between rich and poor, and I am *clearly* rich. Anybody who tells you different does not understand zeroes.

5   Obviously, his definition of rich people is different than mine. So was John McCain's; he came to Orange County and said the rich were people who made over $5 million a year. John McCain's a smart guy and he clearly doesn't understand modern numbers either.

game.[6] Three thousand dollars isn't going to delay my retirement or cause my kid to drop out of law school. But it's a big chunk of change.

And we need to focus more on those three- and four-zero amounts. We need to start listening to politicians and commentators ... and plaintiffs and defendants ... when they talk about numbers, and we need to give some serious thought to how many zeroes we're willing to tolerate.

We need to think about it like it's our own money. When it's our own money, it takes fewer zeroes to get our attention.

We need to re-dedicate ourselves to the three- and four-zero numbers now. And we need to re-educate our colleagues and our children to that re-dedication.

Because as long as there are people in the world to whom $30,000 is a nuisance rather than a year's tuition,[7] as long as there are people who think it's beneath them to work up an honest sweat over $30,000, there will be people willing to run up trillion-dollar national bills.

Frost saw fire or ice. I see numbers.

---

6   That's September 3 for those of you whose value system is so badly warped that you don't recognize the cosmic significance of Cal football. No one appreciates zeroes like a Bears fan.

7   And don't even get me started on the zeroes our billion dollar bagatelles are adding to our children's tuition bills.

Those Shoes

For some reason, the Traffic Safety Administration has decided I do not have bombs in my shoes.

They're right, of course. Hell, it's been so long, I can't even remember the last time I had bombs in my shoes.

And I'm pleased to be able to reward their trust in me on this occasion. I am, at heart, a flag-waver, and I feel good when my government gets one right. It's not a feeling I've enjoyed much of late.

So I regard the screeners who have correctly identified my shoes as harmless leather very much as I would regard a poker player who has successfully called my bluff: I accord them grudging respect. "Yeah, never had that fifth diamond. But I made you sweat a little, didn't I?"

I don't know how they've come to the conclusion my shoes are unarmed. They're pretty big shoes – cowboy boots actually.[1] They're a lot more likely to conceal a bomb than the size sixes of the woman stepping out of her Christian Louboutins a few feet from me.

But the TSA has somehow intuited that my feet are not wrapped in cordite and C4 and therefore need not be inspected.

I know this because they have put me on their pre-screened list for this flight. I'm pulled out of line and re-directed to another – shorter – line. In that line, I am not required to remove my shoes.

And – strangely – that seems to be the only difference between me and the people in the longer lines. I am – as always – required to empty my pockets, remove my belt, display my laptop, and verbally prepare them for the metal clip in my brain, the wire in my breastbone, and the titanium hip joint attached to my right femur – all of which combine to set off metal detectors if I so much as drive by an airport.

I am, in short, required to do everything I would be required to do if I were not one of the chosen people.[2]

This seems like an awfully small perq for all the effort I imagine going into the decision. Surely all the man-hours[3] involved in analyzing the threat-level of my metatarsals could have been spent more productively if all it accomplishes is keeping my boots on my feet. Hell, I'm old, but I can keep my shoes attached to my legs without government assistance.

But, then again, I really don't know what all went into the decision. How do you decide that a person is or is not likely to have explosives where his orthotics ought to be? What is it about me that convinced someone who had never met me, knew nothing of my politics, my

---

1   My dad and uncles were from Texas; having pined for cowboy boots like theirs throughout my southern California Lone Ranger and Gunsmoke youth, I now wear them all the time.

2   Different choice. By a different authority. TSA is not as discriminating and does not impose dietary restrictions.

3   Person hours? Help me out here. What is the acceptable term?

emotional state, or my predilection for Dan Post wides, that the 129 other people on this flight would be safe even if no representative of the United States government had actually eyeballed my socks?

Are there algorithms for such things?

It seems such a specialized choice that I can't imagine it was made randomly. If you send up a pinch-hitter, you consider your circumstances. Do you need a hit, a long fly ball, or a reliable bunt? Would a double play kill you or merely disappoint? Who on your bench has hit this pitcher well in the past? These and a dozen other considerations go through the mind of even a Little League manager in a completely meaningless kids' game. Surely my government factored in at least as much into deciding which dice to roll with hundreds of lives on the line.

Was it my occupation? Surely if that was the key consideration, they could have gone out on a limb and let me leave my belt on.

And occupation would seem to be a really bad criterion. I can name a couple of judges I wouldn't get on an airplane with unless I was assured bodily cavity searches had been performed on them.[4] So it can't just be a matter of trusting judges.

Do they exempt members of the bar? Nope. My wife was traveling with me and she was not pre-approved.[5]

Was it my lack of a felony record? My fine score on my last driving test? My sterling record as a member of the hallway safety patrol at my elementary school?

I don't know. I've spent a considerable amount of time thinking about this – not as much as I spend putting together my fantasy baseball lineup or deciding which Merle Haggard song to use as a ringtone this month, but a lot – and I have no satisfactory answer. Those of you

---

4   The list includes some good friends. Phil Moscone, for example, shouldn't be allowed to travel from his kitchen to his dining room without being checked for instruments of serious craziness.

5   Although, strangely enough, she was pre-screened on another flight and I was not. Apparently TSA reconsidered. I can just hear someone at their underground headquarters in a bunker deep beneath Omaha, screaming, "Bedsworth?! You let Bedsworth through?!"

who have appeared before me have witnessed this process before: the wheels are spinning but there is no sign the gears have engaged.

I have concluded there is just no accounting for the thought processes of my government when it comes to airline safety. They seem to be as random as raindrops.

For example, while I was sitting in my seat[6] going through my ipod repertoire to figure out what to listen to, three very solicitous young women began explaining to all 130 of us how to fasten our seat belts. Really?

Seat belts have been mandatory in automobiles in this country since the sixties. Manufacturers have been putting them into cars in other countries even longer. There can't be a half-dozen three-year-olds in America who do not understand seat belts. And yet no airplane is allowed to take off until we have all been instructed on their use.[7]

Collectively, we have more experience with seat belts than we do with microwaves or garbage disposals, but nobody from the government seems to think I need a lecture before I make dinner.[8]

Seriously, what is the deal with the seat-belt lecture? The security screening just required all of us to remove and replace our belts – some of which appear to require considerably more dexterity than anything we're going to encounter on a 747 – as a condition to boarding the plane. We managed to do that without serious injury or damage to property.

Do they really think the rudimentary buckles on our seats are going to leave us bewildered and unattached? Do they think someone is going to stand up some day and shout, "Omigod, is that how those things work??!!"

I don't know. I try not to throw rocks at the other branches of government.[9] And the executive branch does have a lot of difficult and

---

6   Which, because of the lack of knee room, is becoming more and more like *standing* in my seat.

7   And the flight attendants on our plane were insistent on our attention. If my constitutional law teacher had been as determined that I pay attention, you might have won your last case.

8   If you've eaten dinner at my house, you may wonder about that. I suggest you contact the TSA.

9   I make an exception for Congress. Them, I would happily throw hand grenades at.

varied responsibilities. I would not know the first thing about how to inspect meat or eradicate emerald ash borers or decide how many holograms a $5 bill requires. I respect their broad and important expertise, and I am grateful to them for taking on these tasks.[10]

But I would greatly appreciate it if someone in the executive branch – or even someone in the legislative branch, although there seem to be a distressing number of Congressmen who have trouble keeping their belts buckled – would take another look at airplane safety measures. I'd feel better if there were some sign Leslie Nielsen is no longer in charge.

---

10 Please don't tell the Republican governor who appointed me I said something that could be interpreted as favoring government regulation.

ME AND THE PORN STAR

Catchy title, eh?

I figure by now many regular readers of this publication have stopped reading my stuff because a) it's time that could be more productively spent watching chrome rust, b) it damages their self esteem when their friends catch them, and c) they have run out of synonyms for "drivel" so it's hard to express their disdain for me adequately.

But I know the juxtaposition of bad grammar and the promise of titillation is hard to resist. It got me an appointment to the Court of

Appeal.[1] And it's gotten you three paragraphs into this column, despite your myriad oaths to forswear me forever.

Next month, I'll probably have to use another word like "titillation," snagging those subscribers who think it means something different than it does. Or maybe I can get the editor to change my byline to Coral Carrigan or Edwin Chamaransky or something else deceptively close to the name of someone from whom you would expect valuable content.

But that's tomorrow. In the immortal words of the great legal scholar Katie Scarlett O'Hara Hamilton Kennedy Butler,[2] "Tomorrow, I'll think of some way ... after all, tomorrow is another day."

For this month, I've already got the requisite number of hits.[3] Feel free to move on to the story about the Kendall Winery lawsuit or nine ways to take more effective depositions now.

For the benefit of those of you still reading,[4] there actually *is* a connection between me and a porn star. I don't know what it is, but J. P. Morgan Chase does.

Coupla months ago, Chase Bank opened a branch in my town. It's twenty yards from where I do my marketing, much more convenient than my present bank, so I decided to change banks. I opened a checking account and three savings accounts at Chase.[5]

For five weeks, I made deposits into the Chase checking account – no withdrawals from any of the accounts – and then went in to complain that I hadn't received the checks I ordered yet. They were nonplussed.

"But that account's closed," the teller told me.[6]

---

1   Governor Pete Wilson, who appointed me, turned out to be a lot wilder and crazier than people thought.

2   There's the MCLE portion of today's column: Scarlett O'Hara's full name.

3   For reasons obvious to recidivist readers, I've adopted the Internet measure of success: doesn't matter how long you read, as long as you go to the site.

4   Hi, Mom. Hi, Kelly.

5   Why three? This is how I save money: earmarked accounts. So I needed a "Cait's Wedding" account, a "Golf in Ireland account," and a "Defense of Class Action by Regular Readers of the Column" account.

6   See, that's why they call them "tellers." Because they tell you stuff. More MCLE.

"Can't be," I remonstrated,[7] "It was just opened."

"I'm sorry, sir. It's coming up as a closed account. Are you sure that's the account you just opened?"

"No, I've spent my entire adult life in the public sector and have paid for two divorces and three college educations, so I have so much extra cash lying around that it's hard for me to keep my Swiss and Cayman Islands accounts separate from all my day-to-day walking-around money accounts. Help me out, here; is this the branch where I keep my gold bullion?"

I didn't actually say that, but it crossed my mind.

What I actually said was, "Can I speak to the branch manager?"

The branch manager spoke to me.

While she was speaking to me she also spoke to roughly a half-dozen district, regional, national, international, intergalactic, and transcosmic managers.[8] The information gathered through all this telephonic and internetic[9] conferencing and palavering enabled her to do something I wouldn't have thought possible. Read these words carefully because you will be as stunned by them as I was: she was able to be even less enlightening than the teller.

The teller was at least able to tell me the account was closed. That shed a little light on the "Why haven't I gotten my checks?" question. The branch manager was able to tell me only that it had been closed because it had been determined that I "might be a risk to the bank."

That added not a single lumen to the situation. Doesn't get much more cryptic and less informative than "a risk to the bank."

"A risk to the bank."

Me.

I'm sorry. You seem to have me confused with Ivan Boesky. Or Charles Keating. Or Michael Milken. Or Jesse James.

---

7   All the people who quit reading three paragraphs ago will be sorry when they find out I used "re-monstrated" in a sentence.

8   Hey, if the physicists can get away with this 11-dimension claptrap, I can get away with "transcosmic."

9   Whaddya mean that's not a real word? See footnote 8, *supra*.

I am none of those people. I am an intermediate appellate court judge with no criminal record and no appearances on any no-fly list. Not only have I never damaged a bank, I have never so much as raised my voice – even on this occasion – to a bank employee.

I have an unblemished banking record. I have had an account somewhere since my fourth-grade class opened passbook savings accounts at Great Western Savings in 1956. I deposited my first paycheck, $1.25 I earned working in the school cafeteria, in 1959. I paid my student loans. I've bought and sold three houses, and re-financed several times – always without incident.

And now, after 57 years of completely vanilla banking, I have J. P. Morgan Chase – "a component of the Dow Jones Industrial Average [that] serves millions of consumers in the United states and many of the world's most prominent corporate, institutional and government clients under its J. P. Morgan and Chase brands"[10]– quaking in their boots?!

I, with my $3,200 in checking and savings accounts[11] ... I am a "risk" to a company that boasts on its website of providing 1.2 TRILLION DOLLARS in credit last year? I, a guy who writes six checks a month, am a threat to a company that could buy Bolivia just by taking up a collection of pocket change at its next board of directors meeting?

Obviously, the Chase people have intuited I am capable of much more sophisticated financial machinations than I have thus far attempted. Kudos to them for recognizing me as the edgy, unpredictable, vaguely dangerous combination of Steve McQueen, Willie Sutton, and William S. Buckley that has always been my own self-image.

But where the hell were they when I was trying to sell that image in singles bars and could have used a wingman to vouch for it? With a little help, I could have pulled off that whole, "When he walks into a room, bankers tremble," thing. I know I could have.

---

10 This is their own description. They are not given to hiding their light under a bushel basket.

11 Fortunately, I hadn't closed my old banking accounts, so $3,200 was all I had asked Chase to hold for me. They probably stuck it in a drawer somewhere.

Now, since Chase refuses – honest, they won't tell me – to explain what kind of a risk I am, or how they figured out I was just lying in wait, preparing to pounce, I have to speculate about what gave me away. I'm left to guess what it was about me that put them wise to my nefarious ways – ways I had successfully hidden from a dozen other banking institutions.

I was completely baffled until I learned that Chanel Preston had suffered a similar experience. According to CNBC.com, "Preston recently opened a business account with City National Bank in Los Angeles. When she went to deposit checks into the account days later, however, she was told it had been shut down due to 'compliance issues.'"

Wow, I thought. That's just what happened to me. Right down to the spectacularly unilluminating explanation. This is just what I needed: a precedent right on point.

So I read on to find out why Chanel Preston had been thrown out of City National as unceremoniously as I was thrown out of Chase. Well, it turns out Ms. Preston was bounced because of her occupation. She is a porn star.[12]

That explanation makes as much sense as any. It wasn't personal. Chase just didn't want to be associated with an appellate court justice any more than City National wanted to be associated with a porn star. So all of you who think no one ever listens to your gripes about judges will doubtless be reassured by the fact J. P. Morgan Chase does.

But I feel obliged to point out to those of you who feel this comeuppance is noteworthy only in its tardiness, that Chase hasn't credited *all* your complaints. They seem to agree with you that I'm untrustworthy, treacherous, and ... well, risky. But, like those of you who can't stop reading this column, they can't bring themselves to give up on me entirely.

---

12 Based on the "What's Your Porn Name" game, Ms. Preston's first pet must have been named Chanel and the street she lived on as a child must have been Preston Street. My porn name is Trouble Patronella, which I like almost enough to consider a career as a porn star.

For example, they have no problem with me carrying a Chase Bank credit card I've had for years. A credit card with a $30,000 limit. That doesn't strike them as risky.

Honest. They let me keep my credit card with access to ten times as much cash as the accounts they closed.

I should have gone into banking. Or porn. Apparently neither of them requires as much logic as my present job.

SOFA KING LOW!
(SO FUH-KEEN LOW!)

BEWARE: ERRATIC JUDGE AT WORK

Alright, class, let's review.

When last we met, we discussed Australian trademark law.[1]

Specifically, we discussed the decision of the Australian government to allow a snack food company to market their nut products as "nuckin futs." Some of you – who inexplicably read the entire column while sober – may remember I was disappointed by Australia's conclusion that the first part of this "obvious Spoonerism" had become such a

---

1   Remember this phrase: "Australian trademark law." That's the answer if someone whose approbation you value asks what you're reading right now. If it's someone you don't care about, the answer is "Bedsworth."

"universal" part of Australian life that the phrase "nuckin futs" was no longer offensive.[2]

I was – and remain – concerned that Australia has unnecessarily conceded a coarsening of the level of daily discourse that just can't turn out well. I've reluctantly concluded – "reluctantly" because I like wordplay as much as the next guy and generally reserve my shock and outrage for more than coarse language – the Aussies have made a mistake. I think they'll regret letting that word get its foot in the daily dialogue door.

As I think we would if we made that mistake. If it's good enough for food wrappers, it will soon slide down the slippery slope into movie trailers and ESPN interviews. Eighth-graders will insist on using it in their papers on First Amendment freedoms. Eventually, I will have to find a new word to use when I'm really unhappy about something because that one won't have the clout I'm looking for. "You kids get off my spanarkling grass!"

On the other hand, the British government has taken my side on this issue. They have stood up on their collective hind legs and refused to accept profane advertising.

It should come as no surprise to you – if you are familiar with judges – that this upsets me, too. I am unhappy with the Aussies for not being strict enough about trademarks and advertising phrases, and unhappy with the Brits for being too strict.

Typical judge; nothing ever pleases them.

Let's explain how I can excoriate one commonwealth government for being crude louts and another for being priggish bluenoses on the same issue. How is it *neither* of their opposite rulings pleases me? Then we'll move on to the MCLE portion of today's discussion.

There is a furniture retailer in England called Sofa King. They've been operating for almost a decade in Northampton. Throughout this time,

---

2   Although they did require that the futs in question not be marketed to children – a prophylactic measure I regard as having as much likelihood of success as requiring a warning label on bottles of beer that says, "This product may make you laugh and kiss strangers even while your favorite sports team is getting thoroughly shellacked. Use with care."

they have used an advertising slogan which has apparently escaped attention. The slogan: Sofa King, where our prices are always Sofa King low."

For nine years, no one objected to this slogan. People took their trade to Sofa King, their ads ran in daily newspapers, and the company prospered.

Then someone in the British government spoke the slogan aloud. Our prices are Sofa King low. Sofa King low. Sofa King low.

Now let me warn you ... if you are offended by coarse language ... if you thought last month's column was too racy[3] ... if you've managed to write briefs all these years without developing an interest in the development of word usage,[4] then stop reading right now and do not, whatever you do, repeat the Sofa King slogan out loud yourself. Especially don't repeat it out loud five times rather fast in the company of friends.[5]

Because if you do that, you – or your friends – are liable to hear what it is that caused the British government, after nine years, to holler, "Whoa! You can't say that!"[6]

Outraged, the Queen's minions have descended on Sofa King like the armies of Saladin. Wielding red pens rather than scimitars, they have forced Sofa King from a battlefield scarlet with advertising gore

---

3   This *was* a concern I had. But no one – not one single reader of any of the publications in which it appeared – objected to the subject matter of the column or my treatment of it. Which may indicate either that the Aussies were right about what's become acceptable language or that my audience sets the entertainment bar so low it is indistinguishable from a speed bump. But lawyers are all about words, so I figured this was suitable for an audience of such adults. If I've misjudged your personal tolerance for such subject matter, I apologize.

4   Kinda colored the argument there, didn't I?

5   I ran this by several colleagues at the Court of Appeal. You will be happy to hear that none understood the objectionable nature of the phrase when they read it, and a couple were etymologically pure enough to have trouble seeing the problem even when it was read out loud to them. Which suggests to me that either the Aussies underestimated the gentility of Australian common speech or California Court of Appeal justices operate on a higher level than Australian busdrivers, beekeepers and bandleaders.

6   Or whatever it is the Brits put at the beginning of their Cease and Desist orders.

and ordered bowdlerization[7] of the Sofa King effective ads that have run for nine years.[8]

I think that's wrong. I think they should have just ignored the ads – as everyone had for almost 3,000 days. Yeah, a few folks with good ears might be offended, and a few 12-year-olds might snigger, but basically, no harm would be done. Non-problems, like vampires and yetis, can be handled with non-solutions.

And if that seems to you inconsistent with my nuckin futs position, you are ready for the MCLE portion of the column. To wit:

When I started my career as a young prosecutor back in the Pleistocene, I often sought advice from more experienced prosecutors about judges. It often came in the form of one-word descriptions.

One of the most common was "consistent." This sounds positive and was in fact meant to be. This was the descriptor applied to judges who usually ruled in favor of the prosecution. These were the "good judges."

Then there were the "bad judges" – the ones who didn't consistently rule in favor of the prosecution or, worse yet, tended to side with the defense. These were the judges who HAD seen a search they didn't like or a defendant worth taking a chance on.

Then there was the third category: "erratic." As you might imagine, I didn't expect much of the judges described to me as "erratic." That is a word commonly used in a pejorative sense, and that was how I understood it. Indeed, that is how it was meant.

But I learned after awhile that some of the best judges I appeared before were the ones described by my prosecutorial colleagues as erratic. They were the ones who couldn't be counted on to "consistently" agree with the District Attorney's Office. They were the ones who analyzed each case on its own facts, didn't always accept my analysis of the case law as gospel, and sometimes ruled against me.

---

7   Thomas Bowdler, eighteenth-century rich guy who tried to improve upon Shakespeare by expurgating its "vulgar parts."

8   I have no idea who wrote that paragraph. The phrase "demonic possession" comes immediately to mind.

They were, of course, wrong on the occasions when they ruled against me. But I came to learn it wasn't so much a matter of being "erratic" as it was not accepting me ... or the District Attorney's Office ... or the Attorney General ... or the law firm whose name partners were veterans of the Battle of Hastings ... as the be-all and end-all of legal analysis. It was a matter of doing the job they had been hired to do, regardless of the outcome. And the devil take the hindmost.

The oft-misquoted line of Emerson is, "A foolish consistency is the hobgoblin of small minds." Those first two words are too often forgotten. Consistency is a good thing; *foolish* consistency – consistency for its own sake, and without regard to equity and fairness – is for smaller minds than we need on the bench.

The best judges come to each case with an open mind. They require convincing about which precedential box their case fits into. The best judges are hard to predict and are "consistent" only in the hard work they put into their cases.

Me ... I'm just erratic.

Dopes and Robbers

Woody Allen's classic comedy *Take the Money and Run* includes a ROFLMAO scene in which poor Woody hands a teller a holdup note that is supposed to say, "Please put $50,000 in this bag and act natural. I'm pointing a gun at you." But the teller can't read the word "gun." Woody's handwriting is so bad the teller thinks Woody's pointing a "gub" at him and wants to know what a gub is. The holdup goes downhill from there, plumbing a new nadir – and another laugh – every 10 seconds.

Crime is generally not funny. But specific crimes – like Woody's – can be. And they are always worth reading about. The way our species

– by all appearances the smartest one on the planet – manages to invent new screwups almost hourly is a source of constant amazement, and the chronicle of those screwups is police reports. Reading them is an undervalued perk of time spent in the criminal law.

This is especially true if you learn to approach every police report as if you might be picking up lost correspondence between Mark Twain and Alexander Pushkin.

Because often you are. Or at least it's equivalent.

You never know whether a police report is going to be Flaubert, Stegner, Thurber or Vonnegut, but if you have a deskfull when you come back from court, you can count on something illuminating the human condition with material those guys would have killed for.

Granted, the writing won't be up to the standards of the aforementioned authors. Police officers hate being cooped up in a room writing; that's why they became police officers. One of the few downsides of prosecution is that you have to spend a lot of time explaining to jurors that some of the mistakes in the police report are probably attributable to the desperate desire of its author to finish it so she could get back out on the street.

But not even J. K. Rowling on her best day could match the imagination of the criminal class. Some truly amazing stuff goes on out there. A few years ago, *The Times* of London gave me their "Judicial Wisdom of the Year Award" for concluding – in regard to a smuggling case I wrote about – that "There is no non-culpable explanation for monkeys in your underpants."

I got the props, but I didn't think up the crime. A criminal did.

The criminal imagination is no less astonishing than the Mystery of the Trinity or the acting career of Arnold Schwarzenegger. And if you weren't raised by kleptomaniacal werewolves in lower Manhattan, the facts related in police reports will almost surely beggar your own imagination.

When I was a prosecutor, we had a case involving the holdup of a gas station in Westminster, California. The would-be holdup-man[1] drove in, pulled out a thirty-ought-six hunting rifle and demanded cash from the startled attendant.

This was back in the day when there *were* attendants. Younger readers will just have to use their imagination to understand that back when dinosaurs roamed the earth, you could pull into a gas station and a person – an *attendant* – would greet you, put gas in your car, check your water and oil, wash your windshield, collect your payment, and bring you your change.[2]

A huge meteor struck the earth and killed off all the gas station attendants, so now you only know about them through books and old geezers who write columns. But, as the late, much-lamented Ed Lascher would say, I digress. This is part of geezerhood.

So meanwhile, back at the ranch ... the W-B H-M[3] pulled out his rifle and demanded cash. This was a pretty good indicator we were not dealing with a criminal mastermind here. Passing motorists might not see a pistol, but a guy with a hunting rifle trained on the gas station attendant is hard to miss. Witnesses to the crime were not hard to find.

But cellphones had not yet metastasized into ubiquity, so it took awhile for people to find payphones and call in the crime. Our hero had time to order the gas station attendant to scoop up all the cash at the pumps (yes, Virginia, there were cashboxes at the pumps[4]) and then marched him into the office, where he had the attendant fill his other hand with all the cash in the till.

He then pointed his rifle at the terror-stricken attendant and demanded to know, "Where can I lock you up?"

---

1   The reason for this awkward circumlocution will become apparent shortly.

2   For nothing. Not even a tip.

3   Would-Be Holdup-Man. You forgot that quickly?

4   It begins to occur to me that younger readers are gonna find a lot they don't understand in this story. If you're under 40 and just blundered into this column without noting its title (which the Surgeon General requires me to put on every one), you might just want to skip back to Public Notices; they're usually more entertaining than I am, anyway.

The true answer was "Nowhere." There was simply no room in the gas station that could not be opened from the inside. But watching a hunting rifle shaken at him by a W-E W-B H-M[5], the attendant correctly surmised that was not a good answer.

So he lied. "The ladies room," he blurted.

The W-E W-B H-M put the gun barrel in the attendant's back and prodded him to the ladies room. He then shoved him in, slammed the door, and ran to his car.

Leaving the bewildered attendant standing in the ladies room with two handfuls of cash.

I have often tried to imagine that moment when the wild-eyed would-be holdup-man realized he was only a W-B H-M rather than an *actual* H-M. I've never succeeded to my satisfaction.

But what made him a legend in our office was not so much the fact he drove off without the cash, but the fact HE CAME BACK TO GET IT.

Honest. Westminster PD had just rolled up when the guy pulled back into the gas station. The bewildered attendant, who, according to the police report, was still holding the cash, pointed to the car and said, "That's him."

The guy now realized there were police on the scene and roared away, but he was stopped before he got a block. This was a police report that deserved a Pulitzer.

Some of us were actually somewhat concerned that trial of the case might be problematic. There's an old adage that laughing juries don't convict, and we had visions of this jury being on the floor. *We* certainly were.

But it turned out counsel decided that the defense of, "I just happened to drive into that gas station minutes after a holdup in the same model car as a robber who looked just like me and I just happened to have a hunting rifle too and I drove away fast because I suddenly realized I had a full tank and a pressing appointment," was a low-percentage play. So we never found out.

---

5   Wild-eyed.

I had always assumed forgetting the money was a rare – if not unique – robbery fact pattern.

But then I read about Clifton Taylor. Clifton Taylor lives in Kansas City. Well, actually, he is presently a guest of the United States Corrections Department in Cameron, Missouri, but he *used* to live in Kansas City.

Back in March, Clifton walked into a Kansas City bank and handed the teller a note demanding $3,000 "or somebody out here get shot." Resisting the temptation to initiate a conversation with Clifton about syntax, she gave him $2,700, correctly intuiting that Clifton would not count it.

He fled. With the money.[6]

Unfortunately, part of Clifton's brilliant escape plan[7] was to change his appearance by shedding his black jacket and green knit cap. He figured police, looking for a man in a black jacket and green knit cap, would be completely baffled by his white t-shirt and cap-free head.

He tossed the jacket and cap into the back of a pickup truck. As you might imagine, people seeing a man "running like hell" and tossing clothing into a pickup truck as he ran by, called police. Others chased him from the bank.[8]

Nonetheless, Clifton might have escaped punishment had he not chosen to "lose himself in the crowd" in an electronics store. There Clifton became the star of one of the great moments in cinematography.

Seeking to be as customer-like as possible, Clifton grabbed a phone, walked up to the counter and announced he would like to buy it. Then, as the store's security camera recorded the incident, he reached into his pocket for his newly obtained cash, and found ... nothing.

The $2,700 was in the pocket of the jacket he had shed as part of his brilliant escape plan.

---

6   Which put him slightly ahead of my gas station robber. A lead he quickly relinquished.

7   Most of which can be summed up in the words, "Run like hell."

8   Turns out if you rob a bank *without* a gun, people are more likely to follow you than if you rob a bank *with* a gun. This detail was tragically unaccounted for in Clifton's brilliant escape plan.

So the store security camera recorded Clifton first putting his hands to his head in a classic pantomime of shock, and then lowering his head to the glass display case in agony. As my friend Kevin Underhill put it, "Let's say you're in acting class and you are asked to convey the emotions of a man who has just realized he left $2,700 of stolen money in the coat he threw away while escaping. This is what you should do."

Had Clifton been represented by counsel, the case would have been plea-bargained. For almost anything. Witnesses ID'd him, his DNA was on hairs found in the cap, he wore distinctive designer boots and jeans which showed up rather nicely on the security tapes of both the bank and the electronics store ... the case was unwinnable. It cried out for a negotiated plea.

But Clifton represented himself. Probably not the best choice, but, as the *Kansas City Star* noted, "His judgment had been suspect before."

Clifton's defense was simple: "I think all the evidence was planted and all the witnesses were coached," he argued.

Unfortunately, none of the accounts I've been able to track down relate Clifton's explanation for the one last odd but vaguely incriminating detail in the case against him. His post-arrest interview with the police was videotaped. At one point in the questioning, the detective left the room to get coffee for them.

While he was gone, the camera caught Clifton trying to eat the detective's interview notes.

I wonder if Clifton has relatives in Westminster.

Interactive Urinal Cakes

Yep, that's what it says.

Interactive urinal cakes.

Three words you never thought you'd see juxtaposed. Three words that will make it very difficult for you to live up to last month's vow never to read my stuff again.

Heck, for a lot of you, the juxtaposition of any *two* of those words seems problematic. "Interactive cakes" *of any kind* are hard to imagine[1], and "interactive urinals" seem positively frightening. And a quick

---

1   I, for example, don't want to interact with anything I'm going to eat except by eating it. Even regular cakes should not *respond* in any way to being eaten.

survey of some female friends indicates the term "urinal cake" is not only completely alien but also somewhat disturbing to many women.

But when I explain to them that urinal cakes are the small, disc-shaped disinfectant items placed in the urinals in men's rooms to control odor, the idea those could be in any way "interactive" puzzles them as much as it puzzled me. How could I possibly *interact* with a chemical hockey puck on which other men have been urinating all day?

Well, it turns out it could talk to me. If I urinated in one of a number of bars in Michigan or Colorado, the urinal cake could engage me in conversation.

This may not be news to some of my readers. I suspect there are some in my audience who have often heard disembodied voices speaking to them in the restrooms of bars.

But I am a pretty lightweight drinker; I have never had that experience.[2]

Certainly I've never had the experience of *the urinal* talking to me.

But in Michigan and Colorado, it's becoming increasingly common. And no, it does not have anything to do with the extreme financial straits of Detroit or Colorado's legalization of marijuana – although stress and the cannabial removal of stress were two of the explanations that first suggested themselves to me when I heard about this.

What it has to do with is the efforts of the Michigan State Police and the Colorado Department of Transportation to fight drunk driving. As part of their effort to combat driving under the influence, those agencies have installed in selected bars urinal cakes that talk.

Honest folks, I am not making this up. If I could make up this kind of stuff, I'd be writing for Spielberg and Cameron and the like, rather than Cantil-Sakauye and Baxter and the like.

Apparently, someone noticed that a man who has had too much to drink may be unsteady on his feet.[3] This might cause his stream into the urinal to waiver, thereby betraying his inebriation. Inability to keep

---

2   That's my story, and I'm sticking to it.

3   I hope it didn't take a lot of grant money to conduct the research that resulted in that conclusion.

the urinal stream aimed correctly is probably directly proportional to inability to keep an automobile aimed correctly.

So in dozens of bars in Colorado, men weaving up to the urinal are challenged with a mechanical voice that says, "Keep a constant stream on this urinal cake and let's see how drunk you are."

And, of course, in keeping with the absolute inability of my gender to resist a challenge – especially one that involves their genitals[4] – they try to do just that. The urinal cake then responds to their success or failure by either cheering them as a "winner" or rating their inebriation on a scale that ranges from "Tipsy" to "Uh, where are your pants?"

Of course, "tipsy" oughta be enough to keep them from driving. While I used the common shorthand of "drunk driving" above, "tipsy driving" would be a more accurate description of the violation. You are driving under the influence long before you are driving drunk, and more people need to realize that.

But apparently just reminding men of the problem has a salutary effect. Colorado reports its Labor Day DUI arrests were down more than 10% this year, the first holiday weekend in which the talking urinal cakes were deployed.

The idea that merely reminding men of urination aiming problems can have a salutary effect will come as news to any woman who has struggled with the age-old question, "Why can't he hit the toilet with that thing?"

I think the key here may be the challenge. The urinal cakes turn it into a contest. Maybe if there were targets painted in toilets ... or if "hitting percentages" were reported in the sports pages like batting averages .... But I digress.

The Michigan experience has not been quite as encouraging as the Colorado one. Their approach is identical, but their urine cake is a little more confrontational. It says, "Listen up. That's right, I'm talking to you.[5] Had a few drinks? Maybe a few too many? Then do yourself and

---

4   What, you thought *women* invented the term "pissing contest?"

5   You can just see the guy looking around looking for his interrogator at this point, can't you?

everyone else a favor: Call a sober friend or a cab. Oh, and don't forget to wash your hands."

I like this approach a lot. It sounds like your high school football coach – probably the last authority figure you were really intimidated by – and reminds you of the alternatives to driving. All in all, a nice approach.[6]

And it not only looks out for your safety, but your hygiene as well. Kudos, Michigan State Police!

But, as I alluded to above, they've run into a problem in Michigan that hasn't cropped up in Colorado. Men are stealing the urinal cakes.

That's right. Hard as it is to imagine, men are stealing the talking urinal cakes.

I mean, I can't surmise there is any way to do that other than to reach into the urinal, pull out the ... moistened ... cake, and put it in your pocket. That would seem to me to be an unthinkable thing to do – even if you were way beyond tipsy – unless you thought you had encountered the proverbial talking frog.

I mean, maybe we're looking at urinal cake thefts the wrong way. Maybe the guys who steal these things are so drunk they think they're gonna take these things home and show the wife.

"Look, honey, a urinal cake that talks. Go ahead, Cake, talk. Say something."

Pause.

"Honest, honey, it talks. It talked to me at Muldoon's. Go ahead, Cake, show her. Talk to her."

These are clearly people we need to get off the road and on the wagon. People drunk enough to steal the urinal cakes need to stop drinking immediately, and I suggest to you that the urinal cakes accomplish that end.

I mean, think about it. Surely the thieves didn't put these into their pocket and go back and order another drink. No, they immediately rushed home to show the wife that they had found a miraculous freak

---

6   My God, I'm now *evaluating and rating* urinal cake spiels. My life just gets curiouser and curiouser.

of nature, which would certainly be able to make them rich or grant them wishes or *something* magical.

So even the *stolen* urinal cakes are getting people to stop drinking. And I'm betting the guys who bring home the inexplicably taciturn urinal cakes are enrolled in a program by their wives within 24 hours.

This is a great idea.[7] And I think the Michigan State Police and the Colorado Department of Transportation deserve kudos for giving this a try.

I mean, it cannot have been easy. Guy walks into your office and says, "I'd like to talk to you about fighting crime by deploying talking urinal cakes," your first instinct has to be to give him a breathalyzer exam. And when he passes that, you gotta figure involuntary commitment is the next logical step.

But somebody actually heard these people out. Somebody sat across a desk from the representative of the Acme Talking Urinal Cake Company and thought, "This guy's right. When we arrest these people, we're just treating the *symptoms*. We need to get them in the bars, *before* they start driving, before their driving pattern has a chance to replicate their urine stream. Crime *prevention* is always better than crime *detection*."

And then that person had to carry the idea to his/her supervisor. Talk about taking your life in your hands. This is the career equivalent of charging a machine gun nest. "Boss, I think talking urinal cakes might be the answer ..." is not a high-percentage career advancement gambit.

Law enforcement people tend to be conservative. Theirs is a serious business and they take it seriously. You can pitch talking urinal cakes to the creative director at Hallmark Cards or a partner at Sterling Cooper Draper Price, knowing they expect you to come up with off-the-wall ideas occasionally.

But law enforcement brass hats do not expect that much ... creativity. It took courage to buck this idea up to the next level. I hope it's

---

7   Said the guy who thought ESPN would be a bust and the cellphone was "much ado about nothing."

rewarded by future success in these programs and their enactment in other states.

It would be nice to have someone to talk to in the men's room who was concerned about my safety and hygiene.

THE PARABLE OF THE WOLVES AND FISHES

Raising my consciousness is a herculean task. Most of my friends will tell you it can't be done without a diesel winch and some seriously heavy steel cable. My consciousness pretty much hovers around waist high.

I lived in Berkeley from 1968 to 1971 and saw no evidence that getting your mind higher was a worthwhile endeavor. And the smoke made my eyes water. So I've pretty much let my consciousness seek its own level since then.

And I'm reasonably content with the height of my consciousness. My mind is no longer in the gutter[1] and, while I admit to being unable to cope with most Eastern philosophies,[2] I can spell Kierkegaard without needing a spell-checker, and I have been known to listen to music that has no lyrics.[3]

But I'm afraid I am living proof that you can take the boy out of the blue collar, but you can't take the blue collar out of the boy. I read two things this week that convince me my consciousness is still stuck irretrievably in the last century.

Here's the first one. Truckload full of fish being driven through Irvine, the town next door to mine. Sixteen hundred pounds of fish on their way to becoming seafood. Truck gets broadsided at Walnut and Yale, flips over, and the future seafood becomes future fertilizer. Legions of fish die like Spartans – Spartans in the middle of an intersection 8,000 miles from the nearest Persian soldier.

Okay, you went to law school. What questions come to your mind? You wanna know who caused the accident, right? Is the trucker or the other driver responsible for the loss of the cargo of fish?

You wanna know whether the fish were insured, right?

You wanna know whether the terms of delivery were FOB shipping point or FOB destination. If they're marine fish you want to know whether we're using incoterms[4] or standard freight usages.

And, of course, you wanna know who pays for the memorial plaque for the dead fish.

Yeah, I missed that one, too. The plaque.

What plaque you now – belatedly – ask? The plaque for the fish, man. It's the 21st century; fish got rights.

---

1   Although that may just be a function of the aging process. Men my age have no more success with gutter-thinking than dogs have with car-chasing. And we look worse with our tongues hanging out.

2   No, William James and Charles Sanders Peirce are not Eastern philosophers. I'm talking Indian and Asian Eastern. Try to keep up, here.

3   Though not often.

4   I don't know what they are. I thought you'd know. Your law degree is almost certainly fresher than mine.

Fish got the same right to oxygen you and I and all the non-gill-breathers have. Indeed, considering how hard they have to work extracting oxygen from water, while you and I just suck it in like the spoiled mammals we are, they should have a greater right to it than we do.

So one of my neighbors here in Orange County, Dina Kourda, wants the City of Irvine to install a memorial plaque for the sixteen hundred pounds of fish. On behalf of People for the Ethical Treatment of Animals, she has filed a request with Irvine to memorialize the dead fish with a monument where they died. The plaque would read, "In memory of hundreds of fish who suffered and died at this spot."

PETA says the plaque would remind us "to be careful," "become vegan," and "add tartar sauce to the shopping list." Alright, truth be told, PETA only wants to accomplish two of those goals. I added the third.

I do not make fun of other people's beliefs. I myself am a member of a faith that believes God is a flaming shrubbery whose absolute omniscience somehow did not extend to figuring out He would need a second human gender, thus forcing Him to improvise a jury-rigged woman out of a rib and some duct tape. When you subscribe to beliefs like that, you don't throw rocks at others' glass houses.

So I honor Ms. Kourda's vegan persuasion. But I gotta question the idea of putting up a memorial lamenting the passing of fish who died in an automobile accident hours before we got a chance to slaughter them.

I personally don't eat fish. If it weren't for meat, I myself would be a vegan.

But many of my best friends are piscavores.[5] My wife, an otherwise exemplary woman, eats fish, and I am reluctant to support a plaque that would make her uncomfortable.

---

5   As I understand it, having now used "piscavore" in this magazine, all I need to do is work it into an opinion and get Adam Liptak to put it in the *New York Times* (less of a longshot than you might think; he reads this column) and I have a shot at getting it into a dictionary.

But I must admit it makes me feel vaguely inferior. Humans who can appreciate the value of fish beyond their role as entrees are clearly more evolved than I. And if I hadn't promised my editor a column by tomorrow, I would not make this admission in public.[6]

But it may not even be my most embarrassing admission today. That may be confessing to my absolute astonishment that the State of California is spending federal grant money and a ton of head-scratching over the question of whether the state's ONE gray wolf is an endangered species.

Here's the deal on this one. California had no gray wolves. None. Zip, nada, zilch, ZERO gray wolves. Hadn't been a gray wolf in California in 80 years.

Then a gray wolf from Oregon crossed the border into California. Now we have ONE.

His name is OR-7. The folks in Oregon named him when they put a tracking collar on him. Nice name. Vaguely James Bondian. Not exactly classic, like Rover or King, but nice. Personally, I would have gone with Blitzer.

Crossing the border brought the lone wolf[7] within the jurisdiction of the California Department of Fish and Game, which immediately announced its commencement of a "status review" study to determine whether the wolf is an endangered species.

Hello!? Of COURSE he's endangered. Even *my* faith understands you need to put TWO animals of each species on the ark. A lone wolf – a lone ANYTHING – is endangered. In biology, 1 + 0 eventually equals zero.

But the Fish and Game folks are gonna throw trashbags full of federal grant money at determining whether the wolf should be listed as endangered. Personally, I would prefer it if they threw the trashbags *at the wolf* in an attempt to frighten him back across the border.

---

6   Although admitting something in my column, whose combined readership probably weighs less than the dead fish, may not qualify as admitting it in *public*.

7   I'm sorry; I couldn't resist. I have no will power at all.

In fairness, I'm not sure how many trashbags are involved here. According to the *Huffington Post*, "OR-7 is believed to be the only wolf in the state. The male wolf is outfitted with a tracking tag so he can be studied by government scientists." It may be that his tracking device will save us a trashbagful[8] or two.

But if we could just scare him back north of the border where the other Oregon wolves are, he wouldn't be endangered anymore, and we could put this money to better use. Like fish plaques.

I'm sorry. We're raising tuition and closing courtrooms all over California, but we're gonna spend money figuring out whether one wolf is going to have a hard time reproducing all by himself? I think we'd be better off spending the money on a new left-fielder for the Angels.

Get out the winch and cable, Kelly, my consciousness is dragging again.

---

8   Maybe not as dictionary-worthy as "piscavore," but not bad for a part-time columnist.

A Ticket to Walk

Real, real high on the disconcertingly long list of things I know nothing about is prison administration. Actually, administration of almost any kind is a mystery to me. I can administer first aid or CPR, but beyond that, I have neither talent for nor interest in things administrative.

I do not understand, for example, how I can possibly get paid the same amount as our presiding justice, Dave Sills, who has to do everything I have to do, AND review calendar assignments, referee personnel disputes, evaluate stapler invoices, and choose between color swatches for the re-carpeting of the ladies' room on the first floor. During the 22 years I have been a judge, I have never seen the phrase "presiding judge" without thinking of the closely related phrase, "Second prize: TWO weeks in Philadelphia."

I think people who follow careers in public administration are like people who spend their lives engaged in hospice care or working with burn victims: they are people more capable of tolerating pain and suffering than I. They are people who were chosen by God to do difficult, distressing work because they are strong and dedicated.

Either that or they were puppy-beaters in their last life, and the administrative gig is karmic payback.

Either way, I feel they deserve compassion rather than censure. I try to cut them some slack.

At least I did until I read this: "As a cost-cutting measure, the U. S. Bureau of Prisons has been allowing prisoners to transfer themselves, unescorted, from one prison to another. Officials confirmed that some prisoners at minimum security facilities are given bus tickets and told to make the trip to the next prison on their own."

Honest.

That is a quote from *The Week* magazine, and it was not the April 1 edition. According to *The Week*, we have been transferring federal prisoners between institutions – unmonitored and unescorted – by the simple expedient of handing them a bus ticket and a sack lunch and reminding them to play nicely with the other children.

To the apparent astonishment of the Bureau of Prisons, some of these prisoners have failed to appear at their destination. Who woulda thunk it?

Take Dwayne Fitzen, for example. Dwayne was halfway through his 24-year sentence for dealing cocaine[1] when the Bureau of Prisons decided it was important he be not in Waseca, Minnesota, but in Lompoc, California.

Don't ask me why. It's hard to imagine California had fallen below its imprisoned cocaine dealer quota. My own explanation involves one

---

1   And trust me, folks, you do not get 24 years for dealing coke without some *serious* history.

prison administrator turning to another and saying, "Whaddya wanna bet I can't get Waseca and Lompoc into one sentence?"[2]

So they put Dwayne, a motorcycle gang member known to his fellow inmates as "Shadow," on a Greyhound and said, "Here's the deal, Shadow: you can go spend another 12 years imprisoned in Lompoc, or you can get off the bus ANYWHERE YOU DAMN WELL PLEASE and be a free man until the Bureau of Homeland Security finds you or Osama Bin Laden freezes over. Your choice."

And then, just in case Dwayne didn't fully understand his options, they routed his bus through Las Vegas.

Las Vegas!!! FREE men don't come back from Las Vegas. Men with wives and families and degrees in public administration go off to Vegas and never come back. What could possibly have possessed them to think a guy HALFWAY THROUGH a 24-year sentence would?

Well, as the saying goes, "What happens in Vegas – and Dwayne Fitzen – stays in Vegas." To the surprise of no one but the Bureau of Prisons, Dwayne got off the bus in Vegas and hasn't been heard from since.[3]

It's been five years now, and the Bureau is starting to wonder if they've been stood up.

What prompts me to sing *The Ballad of Shadow Fitzen* after all this time is that the Greyhound Bus people are getting a little testy about being unwittingly converted from a tourist carrier to the underground railway of the federal penitentiary system. After all, even drug mules are given a warning that they're carrying contraband.

Actually, Greyhound's been griping about being turned into a non-televised version of "Prison Break" for some time. All that's new is that the Associated Press just picked up the story and alerted *The Week* and

---

2   A bad idea, but a nice play on words. These public administration types tend to be very clever with words. Justice Manoukian, for example, has degrees in public administration.

3   At least not by anyone at the Bureau of Prisons. My bet is that lots of cocaine purchasers and bikers have heard from Ol' Shadow.

me to the idea that maybe we'd rather take the train than leave the driving to Greyhound and wind up with the seat next to Clyde Barrow.[4]

The Bureau of Prisons can't understand what Greyhound and its passengers and employees[5] have to be upset about. They point out that ONLY A COUPLE HUNDRED INMATES have walked away in the last two years, and, according to prison spokesperson Traci Billingsley, "the savings is substantial."

Well, of course the savings is substantial! It would be even more substantial if ALL of them jumped ship ... er, bus ... somewhere. We could empty the entire federal prison system and the "substantial savings" would be a nice step toward national solvency.

If substantial savings were our primary goal, all we would have to do is route all the transfer buses through Vegas or the inmate's home town, and we would soon be turning our federal prisons into outlet malls and cineplexes.[6]

But somehow most of us had hoped to accomplish a little more with the 36,000 employees of the Bureau of Prisons than turning it into a travel agency for its 204,000 inmates.[7] We had thought, as had Greyhound, that the whole idea of building prisons was to keep these people from showing up at our ballgames and bar mitzvahs and bus stations.

I thought about contacting the Bureau of Prisons about this, but there is a bus line that runs perilously close to my home in Laguna Beach. It occurred to me these were not people I wanted to upset, given

---

4   Of course I know Clyde's dead; all the more reason not to want the seat next to him if you ask me. And all the more reason for the Bureau of Prisons to want to transport him on a bus, since, as an unlikely bus jumper, he would likely raise their batting average.

5   Can you imagine being a Greyhound driver and showing up for work each day wondering how many of your passengers are in fact federal convicts? It would be like working as an usher at Raiders games.

6   Both of which would be lovely additions to the communities of Waseca and Lompoc.

7   Come to think of it, if we've got 36,000 employees for 204,000 inmates – a ratio of 5 1/2 inmates to every employee – couldn't we just give each of the employees a gaggle of inmates, suitably shackled and trussed, and have them take them home and put them up in pup tents in the backyard for the length of their terms? Or would that be too hard on the Las Vegas economy?

the proximity of their chosen method of inmate transportation to my chosen method of eating and sleeping.

Besides, when I looked up Traci Billingsley – the Bureau spokesperson[8] — on the internet, I found a Traci Billingsley (note the spelling of the first name) who had confessed to accumulating 600 Barbie dolls and had a website memorializing this ... uh ... accretion. I have no way of knowing if this is the same person.[9] But I figured it was too big a chance to take.

After all, if I contacted Ms. Billingsley, and – Lord forbid – she *was* the Barbie hoarder, one of two things would happen. Either I would consider her a complete nincompoop, in which case I would be unable ever to get on a bus again until I had obtained a gun permit. Or I would find her not to be a complete nincompoop, despite owning 600 Barbies, in which case my entire understanding of the universe would collapse.

Too much downside.

I think instead I'll just assume the Associated Press got it wrong. I'll just assume the Bureau of Prisons couldn't really be doing what the *The Week* says they're doing. I'll wait to read that the Bureau has sued them both for libel.

And I'll stay off of buses for ... oh ... forever or so.

---

8   Who, by the way, was also their spokesperson on the whole Martha Stewart megillah and is therefore hugely experienced at answering stupid questions and would have been the perfect person for me to talk to.

9   Although it would add weight to my "public administration is karmic punishment for a prior bad life" theory. Obviously, if you come back having to explain the Bureau of Prisons AND with an insatiable thirst for Barbie dolls, you must have been Joseph Stalin in your last life.

I'M NOT SURE I HAVE ENOUGH FOR FRIES!

"CRIME DOES PAY"

Austrian justice and Zimbabwean currency – the world is full of mysteries.

I got a quadrillion dollars for Christmas this year.[1] My wife is so generous, it was a *stocking* gift. Talk about marrying well!

Unfortunately, they're Zimbabwean dollars, and the Zimbabwean dollar has ... well ... kinda fallen on hard times. So the purchasing power of my ten one hundred trillion dollar notes is not as impressive as it sounds.

---

1   Thought I'd start right out with a sentence that's probably never before appeared in print.

In fact, they won't even buy anything in Zimbabwe. In 2009, the government of Zimbabwe just abandoned the whole monetary part of governing. It announced all foreign currencies would be acceptable as a medium of exchange in the country and the Zimbabwean dollar pretty much disappeared – displaced in commercial transactions by rands, pula, euros and Necco wafers.

As I understand it, this happened because the whole "We are not Rhodesia anymore, we are Zimbabwe," thing turned out to be every bit as tough as it sounds.

Imagine changing your name from Smith to Rzepczynski,[2] and you can imagine the problems Zimbabweans ran into. They spent a lot of time giving money to people who looked at it and said, "Zimbabwe? What in hell is a zimbobby?"

What's more, Zimbabwe ran into serious inflation at the turn of this century. Actually, "serious" is the wrong word. According to the Cato Institute, in November of 2008, the inflation rate in Zimbabwe was running at what the Institute called "an astounding monthly rate of 79.6 billion per cent." When the inflation rate is nearly 80 billion per cent per month, "hysterical" seems like a more appropriate adjective than "serious." Even "hyper" seems inadequate.

I don't understand what 79.6 billion per cent per month inflation means. I mean I *literally* don't understand it. I can't comprehend how that works. How can something that cost a dollar on November 1 cost 800 million dollars when my wife's birthday rolls around on December 4?[3]

How do you buy anything? How do you make change? How do you carry it around? How big a wheelbarrow do you have to buy to carry enough money to buy a wheelbarrow?

You order a burger for a million Zimbabwean dollars. By the time it arrives, it costs two million five hundred thousand. You eat the burger and give the guy a five million dollar bill. He brings you back a million

---

2   That's an actual name. Polish I think. Pitcher for the St. Louis Cardinals. Nickname is "Eyechart."

3   I'm pretty sure I'm supposed to buy her something with that quadrillion dollars she gave me.

dollars with the explanation the burger now costs four million. You tell him to keep the change and he tells you there isn't any – inflation just forced the price up again.

This is the kind of economic lunacy I usually associate with bankruptcies and incorporeal hereditaments. No wonder the Zimbabwean treasury threw in the towel and walked away.

The upshot, of course, is that my lovely Christmas banknotes, blue with a bunch of rocks on one side and a water buffalo on the other[4] – and zeroes all over the place – have no value other than as a bright, shiny opening sentence to suck you into violating your New Year's resolution not to read any more of my stuff.

When they fell off the radar screen in 2009, Zimbabwean dollars were worth one septillionth of an American dollar. That is 1/1,000,000,000,000,000,000,000,000 – one followed by 24 zeroes. These are numbers only mathematicians, astronomers, and baseball general managers can comprehend.

I mention this because I think when you read the next part of the column you're going to need to reassure yourself that money isn't everything, and it can't buy happiness, and it's the root of all evil, and all those other clichés you resort to when you read about someone undeserving getting rich. Just pretend as you read the ensuing paragraphs that we're talking about Zimbabwean dollars.

Here's what it said in *The Week* magazine, a mainstream publication not given to stories about alien abduction, conspiracies to elect Kenyans to the Presidency, or CEOs whose salaries are commensurate with their value: "Bank robber has last laugh."

That was the hook. That got my attention just like the quadrillion dollar Christmas present snared you a few minutes ago. The story went on to quote the *London Daily Mail* – another mainstream publication – to the effect that, "An Austrian court has ordered that stolen cash be

---

4   Honest. Rocks. Four or five rocks, stacked one on top of another. And the other side has a water buffalo and a waterfall. My understanding is that the ten trillion dollar note had watercress and a water pistol.

In fairness, Zimbabwe had just emerged from years of oppression as Rhodesia; they didn't have a lot of admired old white heads of state to put on their currency.

given to a bank robber because it 'can't find anybody else to take the money.'"

So help me, that's what it says. They gave the money back to the bank robber. True story. If I could make this stuff up, I wouldn't need to read your briefs and the Supreme Court's opinions. I'd be writing screenplays for Spielberg and Cameron.

According to *The Week*, an Austrian bank manager named Otto Neuman absconded with $240,000 in cash and gold bars in 1993.[5] By the time Interpol – or La Surete or James Bond or whoever the FBI-less Euros count on to investigate bank heists – caught up with him, only $82,000 and some gold could be recovered.

So the question was, "Who gets the recovered loot?"

"Not us," said the bank. "Insurance paid us."

"Not us," said the insurance company. "All we get back is what we paid out, and the gold you recovered has gone up so much in value that it more than covers our loss."

"Us!" said Neuman's lawyer, "Give it to us."

"Okay," said the Austrian court. "That makes sense. We order the money returned to the bank robber."

"What?!?!!?" said everybody else on the planet, "Are you *kidding* us? You're giving the money back to the bank robber because you can't figure out who *else* to give it to?"

"Give it to me. Give it to charity. Give it to Tiny Tim and Bob Cratchit. Give it to millions of poor Rhodesians stuck with worthless hundred trillion dollar pictures of rocks and water buffaloes."

"But for crying out loud, don't give it back to the bank robber."[6]

Actually, in fairness to defense counsel, he not only did not immediately suggest they give the money to his client, he was flabbergasted when they told him they were doing it. Said attorney Herbert

---

5   Kinda hard to get excited about something with only four zeroes while I'm fondling my $100,000,000,000,000 Zimbabwean bank notes. But I'll give it a go. After all, you've read this far, you deserve some kind of return on that investment.

6   This is why they don't let me write too many dissents. I tend to get a little worked up over perceived injustice.

Eichenseder, "I really didn›t believe what the court were telling me but I checked it and it was correct."[7]

Bless his heart, the guy called both the bank and the insurance company before contacting his client. Unlike the Austrian court, this man's grasp on reality was so firm that he was convinced a mistake had to have been made somewhere. He was confident a few phone calls would clear it up.

He was incredulous when he was assured by all involved that no one was claiming the money, and that the only solution anyone could come up with was that it escheated to his felonious client. I dare say his client was as dubious about the news as people were when first told a zimbobby was a country and the money with the rockpile pictures was actual cash.

But according to a dozen news outlets, he took the money.

If you're a Republican, this is just more proof that the socialist European model President Obama is dragging us toward is lunatic. If you're a Democrat, this is just more proof that the rich have so much money they actually – *literally* – don't know what to do with it.

If you're me, this is just more proof that the whole danged planet is going to hell in a handbasket. To paraphrase my southern forebears, "Save your Zimbabwean money, boys, the South is gonna rise again."

Me and my quadrillion dollars (Zimbabwean) will be ready when it does.

---

7   Apparently, because the Austrian court involved was a panel, attorney Eichenseder referred to it in the plural. We approve.

THE BAR NEXT DOOR TO HEAVEN

"A strip club owner was not liable to a man landed upon in an alley by an apparent employee of the theater who jumped from a second story window, the Court of Appeal held yesterday."

That's what it said in the *Los Angeles Metropolitan News*. Honest. This was a case that *other* Court of Appeal justices got to handle. Probably because they knew they didn't dare give it to me.

Actually, the reason it didn't come to me is that it arose 400 miles away from me in your neighborhood, San Francisco. But tell the truth – if this case had come up in my jurisdiction, would you have had the nerve to allow me to write the opinion?

I mean, the guy was injured when someone jumped out of the second story window of an adult theater and landed on him. To me, this has "act of God" written all over it. Especially since the adult theater was called "Heaven." So I'm probably not the right choice as the opinion's author.

But even I have to acknowledge that the contrary position is based on solid precedent. Ever since *Byrne v. Boadle* in 1863[1] we've known there are some things that just don't happen without negligence. People falling out of the sky and landing on you certainly seems like one of those things.

And if Abel Boadle was responsible for the injuries suffered by Joseph Byrne when a barrel of flour dropped on him from the second story of his grocery, why wouldn't the owners of the Heaven Mini Theater be responsible for injuries suffered by Bruce Cearlock when Richard Lund fell on him from the second story of their building?

See how difficult this Court of Appeal gig can be? Here are two completely irrefutable arguments that seem diametrically opposed. And yet ... and yet ... a Court of Appeal, made up of three people wiser than I,[2] was able to sort this one out.

The facts that became *Cearlock v. Lambertson* arose when police went to the Heaven Mini Theater to talk to a doorman who was alleged to have pepper sprayed patrons.[3] The manager, who was talking to his lawyer on the phone when the police arrived ....

Wait a minute ... hold the phone ... let's dwell on that for a moment.

The manager of the adult theater was *on the phone with the establishment's lawyer* when the police arrived? Now that's some first rate lawyering. "For your retainer fee, you get to maintain an open phone

---

1   Citation? For crying out loud, it's an 1863 case and I'm a 1947 judge. You're lucky I remember the name, much less the citation.

2   I know. Hard for regular readers of this column to imagine, but they were able to find three people wiser than I.

3   The *MetNews* says Heaven was a place where lap dancing and prostitution took place. But I can't find either of those facts in the opinion, so I'm just going to congratulate the *MetNews* on the quality of its journalism and applaud my Court of Appeal colleagues for not getting sidetracked by those things.

line to our office 24 hours a day. When the police DO show up – and let's face it, they WILL show up – we'll be ready!"

Impressive. I'd hire those guys.

So anyway, the manager says, "The police are here," and the lawyer tells him, "Don't let them go into any of the rooms without a warrant." Mr. Lambertson and the other owners of Heaven are clearly getting their money's worth at this point.

But moments after the manager tells police he's the only man on the premises, they see a man in one of the rooms and *ask permission* to enter to talk to him. This is pretty exciting to those of us who love criminal jurisprudence. This is going just the way the Founders of the Republic envisioned when they drew up the Fourth Amendment to protect lap dancing.

Unfortunately, getting permission from someone who actually has his lawyer on the phone at that moment takes more time than getting permission from someone not similarly encumbered. So by the time police get to the room, it's empty and the window is open. The window is open because Richard Lund – who may or may not have been the doorman in question – has just jumped from it.[4]

Onto Bruce Cearlock.

Let's look at the case for a moment from Mr. Cearlock's point of view.[5] He's standing outside the bar his wife owns. Honest, his wife owns the bar next door to Heaven. Talk about marrying well.

Anyway, he's just standing there when, according to plaintiff's opening statement, "he was slammed to the sidewalk when a man (Lund) jumped out the window of the Theater and landed on him."

Man, that's gotta hurt. I've watched enough television wrestling to know that having someone jump on you from a turnbuckle pretty much takes you out of championship-belt contention, and those things

---

4   If you've ever tried to close a window after jumping from it, you know that Mr. Lund was not responsible for not closing it behind him, and neither party made such an assertion. My mother would have – she was death on failing to close windows and doors – but neither party here seems to have been concerned about my mother's approval.

5   This is one of the things they teach us at justice school: consider both sides.

are only about five feet off the ground. Having a guy jump on you from the second story ... well, let's just say that probably makes it unnecessary for the referee to start the count.[6]

So that's the case. Mr. Cearlock argued the bar and its owners were liable under respondeat superior and because they helped Mr. Lund try to evade arrest – ultrahazardous activity that called for strict liability. The trial judge listened to those facts as set out in the opening statement and granted a nonsuit in favor of Heaven and Heaven's owners, including Peter Lambertson.

My colleagues on the Court of Appeal agreed. The trial judge nailed this one. Which was remarkable because the case gods seem to have decided it was too easy, so they tossed a couple of astonishingly perplexing facts into plaintiff's opening statement – just to try to throw the trial judge off his game.

First, Mr. Cearlock's lawyer had to admit he had no proof Mr. Lund was an employee of Heaven. They *thought* he was; he had been seen hanging around there a lot; but "there were no records showing who was working at the Theater that night because the Theater did not keep such records" so counsel did have a slight proof problem in that respect.

After all, r*espondeat superior* generally requires that the superior be respondeating for something done by one of his agents. Cearlock's proof about Lund's agency at the theater was less than crystal regarding who – if anyone – was responsible for his actions other than him.

To make up for this lacuna, Cearlock offered to prove that Lund *was* a doorman by trade – presumably to make it more likely he was the doorman at Heaven.[7] How? By proving that his wife had hired him as a doorman for *her* bar AFTER he fell on her husband.[8]

Mrs. Cearlock fired Lund as soon as she found out he was THAT Richard Lund. And how do you suppose she found out? I like to think

---

6   Apparently didn't do much for Mr. Lund, either. Police caught him a couple blocks away despite what must have been a significant head start. I'm betting he was not making good time.

7   Interesting theory. Propensity evidence? Habit and custom? Not sure how this works.

8   Curiouser and curiouser. Can you imagine the poor trial court judge trying to keep his eye on the nonsuit ball through *that* plot twist?

her husband identified him. "Excuse me, I have to get down here on the floor and look up at you to see if I recognize your butt. Yep, that's him; fire him, Honey."

I suspect other employees have been fired for jumping on the owner's spouse, but Mr. Lund has to be the first fired for doing so from a second story window. Not sure what FEHA would have to say about that.

But I am sure what my colleagues at the First District Court of Appeal said about this case. They said *respondeat superior* only applies to torts committed by employees in the scope of their employment. I read that to mean they did not believe jumping out of windows onto passersby was within the scope of employment of *anyone* employed by the theater. So whether Lund was the doorman or not is irrelevant, and the mystery of Heaven's employment records will – like the Trinity and transubstantiation – remain unsolved.

They also rejected the ultrahazardous activity argument, saying that even if the theater could somehow have been viewed as having aided Mr. Lund's attempted escape from the police, "Assisting another in evading the police is an activity that can take many forms, may of which will pose no general risk to the public at all, and all of which can be adequately handled, for purposes of liability, under a negligence rubric."

They talk prettier than me in the First District.

Kudos to Henry Needham, Barbara Jones, Mark Simons – and trial judge Wallace Douglass – for not only getting this one right but keeping a straight face. With truth like this, I can't figure out why anybody writes fiction.

The Tyranny of Small Laws

G. K. Chesterton said, "When you break the big laws, you do not get liberty. You do not even get anarchy. You get small laws." And when you break the small laws, some poor judge gets another ulcer.

Before Pete Wilson went walkabout and gave me the absolute best job in the legal system, I had the second best job: trial judge.[1] I loved being a trial judge. It was like being a big league umpire: All you had to do was yell "safe" or "out" occasionally and you got to watch the ballgame for free.

---

1   California Supreme Court justice is the fourth best job. After Superior Court Adoption Coordinator.

But it's not all black robes and bar association canapés. Sometimes it's like driving around all day with a flat tire: You get where you have to be, but you have to go way slower than you wanted, and the constant wap-wap-wap drives you crazy. Most of those days involve "small laws."

Take my friend Bob.[2] Bob agreed to call a traffic calendar for a colleague so the colleague could take a day off and watch his daughter play in a big soccer game. By the end of the day, Bob – whose lawyering career had consisted almost entirely of trying serious felonies to juries – had grown so weary of hearing that "Everyone else on the freeway was going 88 miles an hour that day; I was just keeping up with traffic," and "I know I wasn't going that fast because my tires wobble if I go over 65," that he was contemplating simultaneously breaking a *big* law and a gavel over someone's head.

So when a woman stood up, looked him in the eye, and actually said with a straight face that it was okay for her to drive in the carpool lane because she was pregnant so there were really two people in the car, Bob went for it. Bob figured, "Aw, what the heck. Give her a break." He found her not guilty.

The next day, Bob was front-page news. War, famine, pestilence, and the National Football League were not front-page news, but Bob was.

In the outraged opinion of most of the Western Hemisphere, the quality of mercy had been strained too much in Bob's court. They wanted his head on a plate. If they'd known where he lived, they would have been there with pitchforks and torches. Indignant letters to the editor filled editorial pages for weeks. Pol Pot got better press.

So the breaking of the small law about car pool lanes caused Bob more agida than all the rapes, robberies, and homicides he'd tried in his entire career. His tombstone will read, "Once Bought the Pregnant in the Car Pool Lane Defense." Small law, big headache.

---

2   Bob isn't his real name. I chose Bob because it's easy to spell, a quality I admire in pseudonyms.

The latest victim of Chesterton's Law of Small Laws[3] is a Los Angeles County Commissioner named Thomas Grodin. Commissioner Grodin, like Bob, made the classic mistake of trying to be a human being while simultaneously serving as a bench officer – a feat of legerdemain roughly equivalent to Harry Houdini's underwater straitjacket trick. He should have just let himself drown.

Grodin found himself handling the case of David Grigorian, a 43-year old man arrested, according to the *Los Angeles Times*, for violating the very large law against making terrorist threats against people. Not a problem. Grodin, like my friend Bob, could have arraigned him on that charge while handcuffed in a locked box and sawed in two.

But Grigorian had also violated the very small law which prohibits the possession of certain animals without a permit. When police arrested him, they found "Cheeta," his pet marmoset, in his car.

Yep. Fate had dealt Grodin an unpermitted marmoset case.

All those classes in Constitutional Law and Intellectual Property and Conflicts, all that midnight oil burned trying to distinguish res judicata from collateral estoppel and trying to figure out incorporeal hereditaments? Worthless. Those are all big law cases. This was a small law case.

Very small. [4] According to the *Times*,[5] "In California, people must obtain a special permit to possess marmoset monkeys ... [and] only those who use the animals for educational or professional purposes, such as filming can get permits." Harbor a marmoset, go to jail.

Okay, so how tough can it be? Judging's a piece of cake. The guy's got an illegal marmoset. You fine him, take away the marmoset and ... and ... well, hell ... what does one DO with an unpermitted marmoset?

---

3   And A. E. Kahn's "Tyranny of Small Decisions," a rule of economics which posits that, "Decisions that are small in size, time perspective, and in relation to their cumulative effect may lead to suboptimal resource allocation," a fancier way of expressing Bedsworth's Third Law of Human Dynamics, "Little stuff always causes more trouble than big stuff."

4   The common marmoset weighs less than a pound. And even the somewhat larger buffy-tufted marmoset, which I mention only because ... well, because who can resist a chance to say buffy-tufted marmoset ... weighs only slightly more. So VERY small laws.

5   And I hope they're right because I am *way* too lazy to look this up.

I mean, it's the guy's pet. Unpermitted or not, you can't just take it away from him and toss it to the nearest Rottweiler. Can you?

Well, Grodin couldn't. Bless his poor, frail, human heart, he worked out a plan under which, "Grigorian agreed to surrender Cheeta to Fish and Game officers, who would transfer the animal to a courier who would then take him to Nevada. Grigorian told officials he would pick up cheetah in Nevada and take him to a caretaker in Arizona."

Honest. The commish worked out a court-approved Monkey Disposal Plan – five words and a hyphen never previously juxtaposed in the history of California law.

So Fish and Game picks up the animal and delivers him to a "courier." I love that part. A courier. Folks, I've worked in the California court system for 37 years. In all that time, I have never found it necessary to employ a "courier" to carry out a court order.

Nor have I ever conspired to transport illicit monkeys across a state line. I mean that just HAS to be some kind of federal violation. Where's Homeland Security when you need them?

But Commissioner Grodin, desperately trying to do the right thing for this man and his monkey, arranged a four-party, tri-state monkey-smuggle only slightly less complicated than the Treaty of Guadalupe Hidalgo. There were fewer players – and couriers – involved in the trade that moved Manny Ramirez to the Dodgers.[6]

This was a lot of work – work the commissioner did not have to take on. I'm sure he went home feeling good about himself. He should have.

But, like Judge Bob, his self-esteem was short-lived. A few months later, Burbank police stopped Grigorian for violating another small law – a traffic violation.

Guess who was with him: a) Jimmy Hoffa; b) Joe the Plumber; c) my friend Bob; d) Cheeta the Well-Travelled Marmoset.

If you guessed (d) – the only one that would get him in trouble – you're right.

---

6   Although Manny was represented by Scott Boras, which is like adding a dozen couriers and a train wreck to the equation.

So did Grodin throw the guy in jail? Did he hold him in contempt or confiscate his car or remand him to the custody of Torquemada?

Nope. Commissioner Grodin is a patient man. He gave Grigorian another chance. He ordered him to get rid of the marmoset and to provide proof of such gotten-rid-of-ness in court.

Which Grigorian did, right? Well ... sort of.

According to the *Times*, he showed up in court with pictures of Cheeta "beside a recently dated Mexican newspaper. Red, white, and green decorations filled the background." Obviously, Cheeta was in Mexico, right? Right?

Didn't I see this movie? Didn't I see it several times with several different directors? Isn't this the way the kidnapper proves the victim is alive, or the bank robbers convince the bank manager they have his family, or the Secretary of the Treasury convinces the Congress that the economy is still alive? Isn't this what you do right before the ransom – or bailout – demand?

Not if you're smart. Not if you realize Mel Gibson or Denzell Washington will be looking at the photo. Because if either of those guys[7] – or Commissioner Grodin – is looking at the photo, you're gonna get flogged with your own monkey.[8]

Commissioner Grodin, having been bitten once, was twice shy. He pressed Grigorian about the Mexican decorations, which looked suspiciously like an Olvera Street restaurant. Grigorian folded up like a wooden chair.

Cheeta was not in Mexico, he was in downtown Los Angeles – historically, a fine distinction, perhaps, but legally significant.[9]

So poor Grodin went through the whole megillah all over again. Tears, recriminations, sad descriptions of heartbroken children losing their monkey, handcuffs, perp walk, lockup. But then he brought

---

7   Neither of whom serves in Congress.

8   So to speak.

9   A VERY fine distinction if one studies the history of the aforementioned Treaty of Guadalupe Hidalgo.

Grigorian back into court and let him promise – again – to hand the monkey over to Fish and Game.

And here, so help me, is the last line of the *Times* story. Here is the part that will either make you want to stand and applaud (my own reaction) or rend your garments in despair (an equally valid response). Your reaction to this last line should tell you a lot about what you want out of your bench officers. Do you want brains or heart? Compassion or capacity? Big law celerity or small law tenacity? Here is what the *Times* said about Grigorian's promise to hand the monkey over to Fish & Game:

"He was told to come back next week with actual proof."

That's right, "Come back next week and tell me again you've gotten rid of the monkey."

God bless him, Grodin still hasn't given up on this dipstick! He gave him another chance!

I figure Grigorian will show up next week with a picture of the monkey in a Fish & Game uniform. From the Lesser Antilles.

The monkey will be sporting dreadlocks and holding a Bob Marley CD. Grigorian will be smoking a doobie and holding a sign that says, "Greetings from St. Barts."

At which point Grodin, like my friend Bob, will acquit him once and for all.[10]

---

10 My thanks to Benjamin Shatz, whose obsessive interest in marmoset law made this column possible and will doubtless be the subject of a special Manatt Phelps partners' meeting at about the same time the Grigorian case comes back to Commissioner Grodin's court.

DALAI DRAMA

Go slowly on this one. This one's like ice cream and bankruptcy law: If you go too fast, you get a screaming pain in the top of your head. And if you imbibe too much, you get sick. So the temptation to stop reading halfway through the column may be even stronger today than it usually is.

I am informed today – by several mainstream publications that seem positively gleeful about the pain they're going to cause our heads – that China has published regulations governing the procedures one must follow before reincarnating.

Okay. If you didn't go back and re-read that sentence at least once, if you didn't spend at least thirty seconds trying to figure out what it actually said or what words were missing or how you had misunderstood it, you are in danger of excruciating head pain. You are *already* going too fast.

Either your world is so far out of control that craziness has become routine, or you think reincarnation is a flower. Either way, you need help. And continuing with this column will only make things tougher on your therapist. Stop now.

If, on the other hand, you re-read the sentence that seemed to say the government of an officially atheist nation was legislating rules to govern the transmigration of its citizens' souls and prescribing whether they would live their next lives as Rothschilds or spiders, you can keep going. Just do so with extreme caution. I'm pretty sure reading this story will have the same effect on your gray matter as ingesting lead paint.[1]

First the good news: You read it right. For many of you this was your first reading test since the bar exam, and you passed. Congratulations.

Now the bad news: My thesaurus does not list enough synonyms for "inexplicable" to allow me to adequately relate this story.[2]

It turns out the People's Republic of China includes a bureaucracy called the State Administration for Religious Affairs, a frighteningly Orwellian appellation given China's official position on religion. I mean, I will confess I have *no* idea what China's State Administration for Religious Affairs (let's call her SARA) *does* on a day-to-day basis. But given that this is an atheist state whose official government position, distilled of all the circumlocution, is that religion is crap,[3] I rather doubt SARA spends its time organizing interdenominational picnics and planning bake sales to raise money for ecumenical soccer leagues.

What they *appear* to be doing is smoking questionable substances. Maybe they're investigating Native American religions this month

---

1   Another Chinese export causing headaches of late.

2   And one of them, "inscrutable," will almost certainly get me in trouble if I use it to describe an Asian nation.

3   Yes, it is crass. But it's an honest translation.

and felt their study would be incomplete without peyote. How else to explain this legislation?

They have promulgated rules that prohibit reincarnation without prior approval of the State Administration for Religious Affairs. Honest. And these are not people noted for their sense of humor.

Okay, here is another speed bump for you. To help you slow down and avoid a headache here, I want you to imagine that an elderly Asian man has come into your office. He says, "I'm getting old and it's time to get my affairs in order."

"Good for you," you respond. "Would you like me to help you draw up a will? Put together a trust? What do you have in mind?"

"Well," he says, "I'm a Chinese citizen, and a Buddhist. I think the first thing we need to do is apply for permission to reincarnate."

The only possible response to this is to curse your fate. "Ah, geez! Aluminum siding. My uncle *told* me to go into aluminum siding. I'd be a rich man today, fishing off the keys and reading Carl Hiaasen novels. But nooooooo, I had to do something 'meaningful.' I had to be a lawyer...."

I mean, there's just so much you need to know to fill out the forms. And they're not only in triplicate, they're in *Chinese!*

Applicant's full name (both before and after transmigration of soul).

Applicant's last date of birth.

Applicant's next date of birth. When does applicant intend to reincarnate? (Please note: Permits are only effective for one year; if permit expires before applicant, he/she/it[4] must re-apply and pay new fee plus re-application penalty.)

Has applicant ever previously reincarnated. Did applicant have SARA permits for those reincarnations, and if so, where and when were they accomplished (attach copies of previous reincarnation permits)? If not, why not? (Attach separate page providing valid, communist party-approved justification for any unpermitted reincarnation. Please note: fact permit not required prior to September 1, 2007, is NOT

---

4   I mean, if you're gonna regulate reincarnation, you gotta go all the way and regulate all directions and levels, right?

a valid justification. Refer to *Little Red Book*, Chapter 17, for enlightenment on possible justifications).

Was applicant, in any previous life, an imperialist running dog? Was applicant, in any previous life insane, tubercular, or Chiang Kai-shek?

Will applicant be a loyal party member and citizen upon reincarnation or will he want to play center in the NBA and give us all kinds of *agida*?[5] Has he ever listened to radio broadcasts from Taiwan or bought soybeans from the Americans?

What or who will applicant be reincarnating as? Will applicant be reincarnating as a higher or lower life form? If higher life form, please attach affidavits of five citizens (one of whom must be a government official) certifying qualifications of applicant for higher life form status. If lower life form, please specify species and genus for all except standard spider transmigration.[6]

What is the purpose of this reincarnation? Is there some reason the applicant wants to continue to traverse this vale of tears?[7] Has applicant been diagnosed with masochistic tendencies? Would applicant benefit from some counseling about the benefits of just stepping off the merry-go-round into nothingness?[8]

Where will applicant be reincarnating? Ah ... there's the rub.

Turns out the new law provides that reincarnation is strictly forbidden in Tibet. If you apply for reincarnation in Tibet, they come to your home and squash you like the bug you were in your last life.[9]

---

5   No I do NOT know the Chinese word for stomach acid. Come on, work with me here, people; this is a second job for me.

6   And by the way, do NOT send me letters accusing me of religious bigotry. According to MSNBC, "a quarter of U.S. Christians, including 10 per cent of all born-again Christians, embrace reincarnation as their favored end-of-life view." End-of-life view? Christianity now allows alternative "end-of-life views?" And coming back as George Clooney is one of the possibilities? Maybe I oughta be paying more attention on Sunday.

7   Of course they'd quote Psalms in the application. It's the State Administration of RELIGIOUS Affairs, for crying out loud. Little known fact: Most of the Thessalonians were Chinese.

8   Yeah, well, if you're gonna work in Religious Affairs, you gotta read a little Nietzsche, right? God is dead and all that.

9   The one you screwed up so badly you had to come back as a human.

You see, this is the real reason for the legislation. That pesky Dalai Lama guy keeps popping up in Tibet. And he just keeps embarrassing the hell out of them.

They don't have the *huevos* to just bump the Dalai Lama with a poison-tipped umbrella,[10] so they're trying to legislate him out of existence. By passing this law, they assure that the next Dalai Lama will be automatically in violation of Chinese law and they can arrest him.

Sure they can.[11]

They need to neutralize the Dalai Lama because, as explained by the Communist Party Secretary of Tibet, one Zhang Qingli,[12] he is "ganging up with Taiwan independence forces, the East Turkestan Islamic Movement, Chinese democracy movements, and the Falun Gong in an attempt to establish an alliance aimed at splitting the motherland."

Now there's a threat the world's largest nation should be losing sleep over. Taiwan, the East Turkestan Islamic Movement, the survivors of Tienanmen Square and the New Age Church of Beijing against China. Man, if you thought United States v. Grenada was one-sided, imagine the final score of China v. Those Four.

Nonetheless, the prospect has the Chinese spooked, and the whole idea of the Chinese government trying to regulate reincarnation is so spectacularly stupid it has me wondering if I should take back all the bad things I've said about the spectacular stupidity of *our* government.

No. No, I shouldn't. Not one of them. The folks in Washington give me ice cream/bankruptcy law headaches every day. To quote a famous Chinese curse, "May they all reincarnate in Tibet and get thrown in the slammer."

---

10 And, of course, reincarnation being what it is, that would be of questionable utility, anyway.

11 If it is true, as Lord Acton famously posited, that power tends to corrupt, it must be noted that it apparently also tends to lobotomize.

12 The true evil of the international communist conspiracy can be gauged by their refusal to follow the letter "q" with a "u," don't you think?

THE RUBY LAFFOON RULE

I try really hard not to throw rocks at legislators. For one thing, they have a very tough job, a very boring job, a job most of us wouldn't take unless they'd stopped hiring at the steel mill. For another thing, if you throw a rock at a legislator, you're gonna hit him; they're as defense-less as an animal with opposable thumbs can be.

Near as I can determine, legislators use up all their instincts for self-preservation during the decennial redistricting process. Having successfully gerrymandered themselves into impregnable wards and boroughs cut and pasted into shapes previously known only to God and Gaudi, they are just plumb tuckered out. Their stores of energy and imagination are so thoroughly depleted that when one of their number comes barreling through the Capitol behind the wheel of one of those zombie Cadillac bad ideas they like so much, it never occurs to them to get out of the way. They just press the aye button and get run down like so many armadillos on a Texas highway.

It's pitiful, really, and we shouldn't be laughing at them when it happens. Making fun of legislators for bad ideas is like kicking Cockapoos for being tiny and adorable.

I know that.

But, sadly, while my spirit is willing, my flesh is weak. Try as I might to be nice to these people, they keep serving up column fodder, and I'm just not a good enough person to resist it.

I would rather not say mean things about them. They do a lot of good, and they set my salary. But hey, I got a deadline coming up in three days. And the folks I'm gonna throw rocks at today have nothing to do with my salary. So another chance to rise above my own base personal interests "gang aft agley."[1]

This time it's Kentucky I can't resist. Which is really too bad. I have a reader in New York[2] who has put together something he calls "The Bedsworth Safety Map." It shows the United States with a big, red "X" in every state I dare not drive through because I have insulted them in print. Kentucky was my last remaining corridor to the east coast. Sigh. On the other hand, there were only six states left on the east coast I could safely visit, so maybe it's just as well.

The Kentucky State Legislature is currently wrestling with a bill that would make Kentucky Fried Chicken "The Official Picnic Food of Kentucky." Seriously. "The Official Picnic Food." Representative Charles

---

1   That's Robert Burns. It's from "To a Mouse." The "gang aft agley" part is Scottish dialect for "go oft awry," which is what the poem tells us happens to "the best laid plans of mice and men." Every so often, I feel the need to include something for the benefit of those of you who think anybody could write this column – something to make you say, "Oh, well if you need to waste three years getting a bachelor's degree in English to write this drivel maybe I couldn't do it; my pain threshold is too low. Maybe I *couldn't* write this column."

2   Probably only one. We'd have to appoint attorneys for everyone in the state before questioning them to find out if there are more, so let's just assume there's only one.

Siler has introduced a bill that would so designate KFC's "Original Recipe."

How could anyone expect me not to tee that up? Gandhi couldn't resist a straight line like that.[3]

Neither can PETA. You remember PETA: People for the Ethical Treatment of Animals. They're like the Sierra Club for Cockapoos. They're the kind of organization legislators should have to protect from us rock-throwers.

PETA's very upset that Kentucky is considering "honoring" Kentucky Fried Chicken. They loathe Kentucky Fried Chicken. If PETA were Iran, they would consider KFC "The Great Satan." So they're on Representative Siler like ugly on a bulldog.

Their position, I think eloquently expressed, is that, "If the state legislature moves forward with this one, then they should change Kentucky's state bird from the cardinal to the debeaked, crippled, scalded, diseased, dead chicken." That lovely picture is provided by one Bruce Friedrich, identified by the *Lexington Herald-Leader*[4] as PETA's vice president. If I were a state legislator, with my heretofore referenced diminished capacity for self-preservation, I would not want to run afoul[5] of Mr. Friedrich.

But with all due respect to the formidable Mr. Friedrich, I think PETA's missing the point here. The point is, "How has Kentucky gone 216 years without an official state picnic food?" I mean, I can understand failing to provide health care for its citizens and neglecting the state's infrastructure and not putting up barbed wire all along its borders to protect its citizens from terrorist hordes swarming down from Ohio like so many Buckeye Visigoths ... but how could Kentucky's legislature have shirked its responsibility to designate an official state picnic food?

---

3   Okay, maybe Gandhi could. Gandhi did not have to fill column space every month.

4   "Spanning the globe to bring you the constant variety of sport." Me and *ABC's Wide World of Sports.*

5   Or, in Kentucky's case, a-fowl.

Now I know what you're thinking. You're thinking, "Isn't the mint julep already the official state picnic food of Kentucky?" Well, apparently not. It isn't even the official state beverage. Milk is. They decided that in 2005.[6]

They got lots of other official stuff. They got an official state dance (clogging), an official state butterfly (the Viceroy), and an official state locomotive (Old 152).[7] They've even got an official state silverware pattern, for crying out loud (Old Kentucky Bluegrass: The Georgetown Pattern) and TWO state mottos (one in English, one in Latin, but they're different; go figure).

Yet they have NO OFFICIAL STATE PICNIC FOOD. God bless Representative Siler for straightening that out.

Or at least trying to. There is some opposition to Rep. Siler's bill quite apart from its PETA-antagonizing propensities. The *Ashland Daily Independent*, for example, has editorialized that the official state picnic food should just be generic, unbranded fried chicken. As it cogently points out, "not all chicken served at picnics in Kentucky is from KFC."[8]

Which reminds me, didn't the KFC people *become* KFC by deleting the words "Kentucky," "Fried," and "Chicken" from their corporate moniker?[9] Didn't they make a corporate decision they did NOT WANT to be identified with Kentucky, fried foods in general and fried chicken in particular? Are these really the people the Kentucky State Legislature ought to be honoring?

If California Pizza Kitchen decided to call itself CPK so it could better market itself to Texans, wouldn't Californians be a little offended? I would be. Especially if we'd put a bust of the founder of the company in the state capitol.

Yep, there is a bust of Harland Sanders in the Kentucky State Capitol building. I know this because I almost wrote about it when Pamela

---

6   And wouldn't you want to hire the lobbyist who was able to get milk declared the official state beverage in the state that invented bourbon?

7   Hell if I know. It's a locomotive. What would an English major know about locomotives?

8   Now *there's* an editorial board not afraid of controversy.

9   Or at least "entucky" "ried" and "hicken."

Anderson tried to get the governor to remove the bust a couple of years ago because of her concern about KFC waterboarding chickens.[10] I spent an hour trying to write the column before deciding it was not worth all the effort just for the Pamela Anderson/Colonel Sanders bust/bust double entendres.[11]

So I can certainly understand the feeling of some Kentuckians that they've already done enough for a company that jumped ship years ago.

Besides, there are some disturbing questions raised by some of the **whereases** in Representative Siler's bill. According to the first **whereas**,[12] Harland Sanders opened his first restaurant in Corbin, Kentucky,[13] in 1930. But according to the third **whereas**, Colonel Sanders's "Original Recipe" fried chicken was first cooked in Colonel Sanders's restaurant in 1940.

Which means it took ten years for the Colonel to come up with his "Original Recipe?" I'm sorry, that's a use of the word "original" I – the English major – have a little trouble with. What fried chicken recipe was used for the ten years *before* the "original" recipe? What was the universe like *before* the Big Bang?

If I were Kentucky, I would want answers to these questions before I enshrined that finger lickin' good stuff in my codified statutes forever and ever.[14] Can you imagine how embarrassing it would be to have to stand in Costco parking lots gathering signatures for the initiative to *repeal* your Official State Picnic Food designation?

But the biggest reason not to name Kentucky Fried Chicken the Official State Picnic Food of Kentucky is found in the second **whereas**

---

10   At least I think it was waterboarding. I know it was torture of some kind. I tried to double check with the Department of Justice, but they informed me General Mukasey is still working on that one.

11   And because at that time there were still East Coast states I wanted to visit and I was hoping to keep Kentucky open on "The Bedsworth Safety Map."

12   This word apparently can only be printed in boldface fonts. I went out and looked at a couple of documents I have that contain **whereases**, and, sure enough, boldface.

13   Which, lo and behold, is in Rep. Siler's district.

14   Well, at least the first one. Maybe it is asking a little much to expect the Kentucky State Legislature to explain the Big Bang thing. At least right now while they're gearing up for redistricting.

of the resolution in support of it. It says, "**Whereas** Kentucky Governor Ruby Laffoon made Harland Sanders an honorary Kentucky Colonel in recognition of his contributions to the state's cuisine in 1936...."

Governor Ruby Laffoon?!?! That alone should be enough to keep this bill from ever becoming law. It would violate Bedsworth's Third Law of Statutory Interpretation: no statute that requires an admission the state once elected a man named Ruby Laffoon as its governor can possibly be a real law. Ignore it.

Not a Leg to Stand On

My gender has a hard time with pants.

I don't know why this is. As body coverings go, pants are decidedly low-tech. You would think a gender that can – more or less – cope with shoelaces and French cuffs and half-Windsor knots could manage pants. I mean, once you get out of the way of the zipper, how tough can it be?

And yet, my kind – conquerors of empires, builders of cathedrals, golfers on the moon, architects, and successful defenders of a social structure which prefers them over the other gender in the face of over-whelming evidence of contrary worth – cannot manage pants.

You want proof of this inadequacy? Go to a ballgame. Watch the men walking by with their bellies hanging over their belts. Here are hundreds of men who are convinced their pant size, like their pizza preference, was fixed when they were nineteen and has never changed. Like my friend the high school free safety, they are convinced their waist size is still 34, and – while vaguely concerned about the fact their inseam has somehow shortened five or six inches, leaving their pants legs scrunched up around their ankles like some kind of bizarre, wool-worsted slinkies – they see no reason to change their pants-buying habits.

We need a telethon for these people. Somehow pants have clouded their minds and made them unable to employ the minimal technology represented by a mirror. Even a cat figures out eventually that the picture in the mirror is him. But men don't. If they did, they wouldn't dress like this. Pants do this to us.

Pants have always clouded our minds. What is the question that has historically screwed up men's heads more than any other? What question has every family counselor and divorce lawyer and priest had to address more than any other relationship problem? *Who wears the pants in the family?*

Men are constantly worrying about who wears the pants in the family. This is a remarkable thing, considering the whole planet has been entrusted to us and we're pretty much steering it to hell in a handbasket. You would think we would have more important things on our minds – especially since, considering the ballpark evidence, we should all be walking around in caftans, anyway. But this is the power pants have over us.

Studies have repeatedly shown that there is less divorce in countries where men do not wear pants.[1] This just makes sense. If you don't have to figure out who wears the pants in the family, you have a lot more time

---

1   I'm not actually aware of any of these studies, but I'm sure they exist, so I see no reason to waste time looking them up. This, by the way, which I like to think of as "confident assertion of the likely" turns out to be a very fruitful method of dealing with inadequate appellate records. But my colleagues – *most of whom wear pants* – seem resistant to this approach. Still more evidence of the destructive influence of pants.

to address the real issues in the marriage – like who gets custody of the remote and what is the default setting on the toilet seat.

And it's not just relationships. Pants play havoc with our judgment about everything. Anyone within ten years of my age has known at least a half-dozen authority figures – judges, district attorneys, managing partners – who bent themselves into Gaudi corkscrews, over the issue of whether women should be allowed to wear pants to the office, to court, to depositions, or wherever.

What was that all about? Propriety? Modesty? Bullshorts. It was about pants. Pants turn men's minds to okra. Old, overheated, fermenting okra. Always have, always will.

So I was not the least bit surprised to pick up the May 4 issue of *The Week*[2] and read that "a North Carolina man attempting to pick up his pants from a dry cleaner was arrested for not wearing any pants." Clearly, the man's mind had been overwhelmed by this simplest of pants issues. Clearly, the logic of, "I don't have any pants on now, but once the lady at the dry cleaners gives me mine, I will have some," convinced him he was on firm ground.

Golden retrievers – who do not wear pants – do better than this.

But for those skeptics amongst you who think the guys at the ballpark and the pantsless North Carolinian are some kind of cretinous aberrations, let me trot out Exhibit AA.[3] Exhibit AA is Roy L. Pearson, Jr.

Roy is a judge. Those may be the four most painful words I've ever typed, as you will understand if you read on. If you're already convinced that pants are a bad idea and would like to hold on to whatever illusions you still maintain about the judiciary, turn to the next page and don't give this matter another thought. Not reading my stuff is always a better idea than reading it, and you gotta figure if I'm suggesting it, this is probably worse than most. So stop now and go look at the expert witness ads, which are a lot more entertaining anyway.

---

2   My favorite magazine next to *The Hockey News*. By the way, have you ever noticed that hockey players don't wear pants? They wear shorts. This explains why the players' minds are so much clearer than in other sports.

3   For Absolutely Astonishing.

And yet, here you are, still reading. Either you've lost three straight summary judgment motions and are looking for reinforcement of your low opinion of the bench, or you're just in the mood for a train wreck. Either way, Roy L. Pearson, Jr., fills the bill.

According to the Associated Press, Pearson was appointed as an administrative judge in Washington, D. C., in May, 2005. He immediately did what all judges do when they're first appointed: He took several suits in for alteration.[4] He took them to Jin Nam Chung and Ki Chung, and their son Soo Chung, Korean immigrants who own and operate an establishment called Custom Cleaners.

When he went back two days later, one pair of pants was missing.[5] Long story short, Judge Roy and the cleaners have been unable to satisfactorily resolve the missing pants issue, so he has sued them for the customary sixty-five million dollars.

Yep, that's what it says. Sixty-five million dollars. That's a six and a five, followed by six zeroes and a couple of commas.[6] $65,000,000. American. He sued them for sixty-five million dollars. Over a pair of pants.

That is probably the biggest price ever put on a pair of pants by someone not employed as a purchasing agent for the Department of Defense.

"How," you might ask yourself, "did Judge Roy come up with that number for his damages?" – a question you might immediately follow with, "Was peyote involved?" And while you will doubtless be dismayed to learn I do not have the answer to the second question, I do have the answer to the first. When you hear it, I think it will answer the second question to your satisfaction.

---

4   Contrary to common belief, the head is not the *only* thing that swells on this occasion.

5   If, after all I've said up to this point, you can read the word "pants" in this context without wincing in anticipation of ineluctable pain and embarrassment, go back and start reading all over again. You obviously have not been paying attention.

6   If you were just dealing with me, you could leave out the commas. But Judge Roy L. Pearson, Jr., strikes me as a man not likely to look the other way for bad punctuation.

Judge Roy does not maintain the original pants were worth $65 million.[7] He says the suit of which the pants were half was worth only something over $1,000. He arrived at the ... somewhat larger figure[8] ... by applying what, for lack of a better term, I'll call "pants logic" to the District of Columbia's consumer protection statutes. Here is how that works.

Judge Roy was so devastated by the loss of his pants that he could no longer use Custom Cleaners. There were no other cleaning establishments within walking distance of his home, so he had to drive to another cleaning establishment. Judge Roy has no car. That necessitated renting a car. In fact, it necessitated renting a car every weekend for the two years since his pants went MIA.

Now, if you're like me,[9] Judge Roy has already lost you. You could summary judgment him right now just for making the lunatic rental-car argument, right?

And I've given him the benefit of the doubt. According to all the news reports, Roy wants rental car reimbursement for TEN years. But I figure that has to be a typo. Even if Roy were rolling the pants up and smoking them, he couldn't be asking for ten years' worth of car rentals for two years of pantslessness.

But that doesn't get us anywhere near $65 million does it. No, that's where the District of Columbia's consumer protection act comes into play. According to the AP, "The bulk of the $65 million demand comes from Pearson's strict interpretation of Washington's consumer protection law, which imposes fines of $1500 per violation per day. Pearson counted 12 daily violations on each of 1,200 days[10], then multiplied that by three defendants."

---

7   Although he must have been VERY fond of them, since he's since turned down offers of a replacement suit, $3,000, $4,600, and $12,000 for them so far.

8   The original said "crazy ass number," but my editors prefer that I stay away from technical terms.

9   Don't worry; you won't be required to admit this. It's really only a rhetorical device. Relax.

10   No, I don't know how he arrived at 1,200 days. My guess would be the aliens communicating with him through the fillings in his teeth came up with it.

By my math, that's $64,800,000. The rest I take to be the rental car costs and the $1,000 for the original pants. I tried to double check this with the only two guys I know who have experience with numbers this big but Blaise Pascal is dead and Donald Trump was pretty busy counting his *own* money.

This is the mathematical equivalent of three-card monte. Nobody's done math this questionable since Seward convinced the Russians (who were doubtless wearing pants at the time) to sell us Alaska for only seven million dollars. And Alaska was in mint condition. Pristine. These pants weren't even new!

You know who I feel sorry for? Oh, sure, I feel sorry for the cleaners. And I feel sorry for ANYBODY who has to deal with Roy L. Pearson, Jr., on any level more personal than flipping him off. But I really feel sorry for the defendants' attorney, one Chris Manning.

I have never met Mr. Manning. I have no idea how good a lawyer he is. I have no idea how glib and articulate and intelligent he is. But I know this: I know John Marshall Harlan and Oliver Wendell Holmes[11] working as a tag-team could not explain to Korean immigrants – or anyone else for that matter – how our legal system could allow a 65-million-dollar lawsuit over a lost pair of pants to drag on for two years.

Not without first explaining the ability of pants to cloud men's minds.

If I were Mr. Manning, I'd go for an all-woman jury.

---

11   Either of them. Both of them. "And their sisters and their cousins, whom they reckon by the dozens, and their aunts." Doesn't matter how many people you put on this task, it can't be done.

Two Friends and a Limo

It is difficult to express the dread with which I approached my first colonoscopy.

To understand it fully, you have to appreciate my almost preternatural capacity for dread. I inherited it from my mother, who won the Olympic gold medal in freestyle dread at the 1952 Helsinki Olympics and spent the rest of her life waiting for the phone call informing her she had failed the drug test and would have to give the medal back.

The phone call never came, and Mom's medal now hangs from the rear view mirror of my wife's car, reminding us that a meteor could crush us at any moment. But Mom soldiered on. She spent the rest of her life seeking clouds for every silver lining, somewhat bemused by the fact her existence had not yet been interrupted by what she regarded as the inevitable market crashes, typhoons, and plague outbreaks to come.[1]

Despite what the geneticists may say about it, I have inherited this trait as surely as Secretariat inherited speed from Bold Ruler and stamina from Nasrulla. I dread at a chromosomal level. I am capable of Rooseveltian dread: I can actually fear fear itself. I fear the fear I will feel when I start fearing something.

So when I tell you I was dreading my colonoscopy, it means something. I'm not talking here about ordinary garden-variety bar exam dread. I'm not talking about letter from the IRS asking you to bring with you your tax records for the preceding seven years dread. I'm talking about full-on, under the theater seat with your eyes closed, screaming at Sigourney Weaver not to open that airlock because the scariest monster in the history of the universe is on the other side, thus embarrassing your wife so much she refuses to help you get the jujubes off the back of your shirt and threatens never to go to the movies with you ever again dread.

I did not want to go.

I am told most men react similarly – though less spectacularly. I'm told, for instance that most of them don't actually obtain a false birth certificate and make an appointment to have their fingerprints burned off with acid so they can deny that they've reached the age when a colonoscopy is recommended. And apparently my gastroenterologist had never previously had a patient ask if he could avoid the need for a colonoscopy by merely "putting a cork in it and taking all my meals intravenously for the rest of my life."

But this is clearly one of the areas in which we guys fully live up to our reputation as the "weaker sex." It turns out I can actually whimper; I had no idea.

---

[1]   And meteors. Did I mention meteors?

My buddies didn't help. The procedure apparently includes the injection of some kind of sadism-inducing drug that causes men who undergo it to feel obliged to describe it in terms previously reserved for tales of Civil War amputations and sports cars driven under eighteen-wheelers at 95 miles per hour.

They had me convinced the instrument in question was constructed of Alyeska pipeline remnants – a size required to accommodate the camera, which was "the exact same one they use for the Angel games, you know, the one in the well behind the third-base dugout." And of course all of them knew a friend of a friend's cousin's neighbor who had "had one go wrong."

Fortunately, my friend Cliff Roberts was also a little overdue for the procedure and had decided his fear of his wife was greater than his fear of pain.[2] Apparently Jill had conjured up a parade of horribles about Cliff's life *with* her and *without* a colonoscopy that was worse than the ones Cliff had been able to devise about the procedure itself and so – because of his *feeble* and *inadequate* imagination[3] – he had agreed that HE AND I would have it done.

Presumably the lawyers among you are as confused by this syllogism as I was. It seems to go: Cliff is afraid of his wife. His wife wants him to get a colonoscopy. Therefore Beds is going to get a colonoscopy.

But Jill, who is slightly larger than a fox terrier and, as near as I can determine, knows not a single profanity, was – despite those handicaps – somehow able to convey to me as clearly as she had conveyed to Cliff the absolute necessity of this procedure to my continued enjoyment of life. Suffice it to say Sigourney Weaver would not have opened the airlock if an angry Jill Roberts were on the other side.

Nor would she have done so if it meant she had to prep for a colonoscopy. I will not dwell on this. You all know what I'm talking about, and my editor is utterly terrified by the prospect of me describing it in

---

2   A conclusion only a married man can understand.

3   A character trait inexplicably unremarked upon by any of the many judges before whom Cliff had argued law and motion matters.

his publication. Let's just say I spent an evening taking pills and drinking Gatorade.

Let's just say I slept on the floor of my bathroom because I was unable to take the five steps to my bed without needing to two-step back to the porcelain. Let's just say I can now tell you, should you ask, how many tiles there are on any surface of that room.

And let's have a round of applause for the chemists who were able to put together a drug so powerful that it not only emptied every part of my digestive system – every nook, every cranny, every minute diverticulum[4] — but also somehow sucked into and through my lower tract a collection of unswallowed objects that included my wedding ring, two marbles, and an old Eddie Mathews baseball card I hadn't seen in years.

If we could somehow apply this stuff to U.S. foreign policy, we'd be out of Iraq in a week.[5]

Next thing I know, the limousine is picking me up outside my home at five in the morning[6] to take me to UCLA.[7] Unfortunately, the Amazing Fantastic Intestinal Cleaning Solution is not yet done. We get as far as Hawthorne and have to pull into a gas station.

Now picture this, if you will. It's 7 in the morning, a big, black stretch limo pulls into a Mobil station in a blue-collar, largely African-American neighborhood, and three white people[8] exit, seriatim, go into the restroom, come back and get into the limo and then drive away.

What does that sound like to you? Of course. That's clearly a drug transaction. Any cop worth his badge could have gotten a search warrant for that limo on those facts alone. I think subconsciously Cliff and I were hoping to be stopped and arrested.

---

4 Too few people fully appreciate the opportunity for vocabulary enhancement presented by a colonoscopy.

5 Iraq, Guantanamo, Puerto Rico, the entire Eastern Seaboard, and most of the Great Lakes region.

6 Apparently Cliff won a few cases here and there.

7 Cliff chose the doctor. I can only assume Christian Barnhard, Charles Mayo, and Derek "McDreamy" Sheppard were unavailable.

8 Jill came along to make sure we didn't tell the limo driver to just take us to Vegas instead.

But that was the worst part. The procedure itself is a piece of cake. Or at least, as far as I can remember, it is.

I can't really say this with the same certainty with which I usually pontificate because part of the anesthesia is a drug called Versed – a benzodiazepine that not only relaxes your muscles but also wipes out a couple hours of memory.

In fairness to modern medicine, the level of drug necessary to relax my sphincter five minutes before a colonoscopy is probably so high I'm lucky I can remember anything that happened after my fifteenth birthday. But it is a little disconcerting to expend so much energy being afraid of something and then not even be able to remember it afterward.

And except for being a little groggy, there are no after-effects. No pain, no intestinal distress, nothing. We stopped to get doughnuts on the way home. Sigourney Weaver did not stop for doughnuts on the way home.

Which is my main reason for writing this piece: I want to try to convey how utterly ordinary and routine this procedure is and encourage you to get it done.

I'm a reasonably intelligent guy. And, all kidding aside, having been through brain surgery, heart surgery, and several kidney stones, you wouldn't have expected me to be inordinately put off by the prospect of a colonoscopy.

But I was. I put if off until I was 55. Somehow, the disabling panic I felt whenever I contemplated this particular procedure kept me from doing something I knew I should have. And being a "busy guy" with "an important job" enabled me to keep making excuses.

I don't know how it is for women – Jill Roberts didn't seem the least bit nervous about it – but I've talked to enough of my male peers to know I am not the only one who gets queasy about medical procedures that involve taking off our underwear. And I've actually had to yell at a couple of friends who gave me that "I'm gonna do it soon; I'm just really busy right now" stuff.

So I write this month to say, "Get over it." This article actually recounts an episode of five years ago, and last week I repeated the same benign experience.[9] So I now know I didn't just get lucky five years ago; they're ALL this easy.

This time they added an endoscopy to my shopping cart. They put one camera in from one end and another one in from the other end and stopped when they saw each other. They biopsied stomach tissue. They examined my stomach, my colon, both intestines, my esophagus and my back molars. It was still painless. WE STILL GOT DOUGHNUTS ON THE WAY HOME.

This is a no-brainer. The only way you can screw this up – the only way it can hurt you – is if you don't do it.

So stop making excuses about your calendar. Stop fretting about the firm or the office or the staff. You can do this on a Saturday and not miss a minute of work, so all those work-related excuses ... well, they're all stuff the Amazing Fantastic Intestinal Cleaning Solution will get rid of ... and they aren't fooling anybody.

Stop promising yourself – and your loved ones – that you'll "get around to it" soon ... AND DO IT. Have your "colonoscopy party" and stop worrying about it. Stop being a *busy* lawyer and start being a *smart* one.

Trust me, it's a walk in the park. Do it.

Call two friends and rent a limo.

---

9 Sans gas station visit; prep was much easier this time.

"Start Spreading the News"

My career on the bench has now reached twenty years, but it includes very little family law work. Turns out if you deny just one divorce, they stop sending them to you.

But that is apparently not the rule in other states. Or at least one state. According to the Associated Press, "New York is the only state that won't allow the speedy dissolution of a marriage without proof that one spouse is somehow at fault." God bless those New Yorkers. They know that eliminating fault from divorce takes all the fun out of it.

While the pop standard "New York, New York" celebrates the virtues of making "a brand new start of it in old New York," that does not apply to marriage. If you want a brand new start to *that*, somebody has to take the blame.

There are only six grounds for divorce in New York. Adultery or cruel and inhuman treatment are the first two, but they tend to be literal about the "cruel and inhuman treatment" part. "You don't bring me flowers anymore," apparently doesn't cut it.

It's the other four grounds I find most interesting. They consist of: (1) living apart for a year, (2) living apart for a year, (3) living apart for a year, or (4) going to prison for three years.

Honest, that's what the statute provides. I don't know why. I'm 3,000 miles from New York and there is no one I want to divorce there, so it would be wrong for me to spend a lot of time researching this, but four of the six grounds for divorce in New York are: abandonment *for a year*, living apart under a court-approved separation agreement *for a year*, living apart under contract *for a year*, or one of the parties being imprisoned *for three years*.

I can only conclude from this that the New York State legislature decided, "If we only make 'em go to prison for a year to get out of their marriage, we'll have to hire thousands of additional police; make it three years."

I mention all this so you can appreciate the dilemma of Simon and Chana Taub. Simon and Chana Taub are 57 years old. They are married. They hate each other.

They both want a divorce. But there has been no provable adultery, no cruel or inhuman treatment[1], and neither is willing to live apart from the other because *neither is willing to move out of the family residence.*

So they have been fighting for three years over who has to move and who has to take the blame for the divorce and who should pay the lawyers' fees and what color the sky is and what sound cows make and what day comes before Thursday.

---

1   Remember, just being a world-class schmuck doesn't qualify.

I personally feel they should both be sent to prison for three years and then given their divorce, but that is not the solution the New York courts have come up with. The solution they came up with was to divide the Taub's three-story, million-dollar Brooklyn row house down the middle WITH A WALL.

That's right. A wall.

A trial court, unable to grant the parties – no, that's not the right word – unable to grant the *combatants* a divorce, ordered that they be separated by building a wall through the house. Chana appealed that order.[2] But an appeals panel affirmed the lower court's solution,[3] and last December the wall went up.[4]

Chana and THREE OF THE COUPLE'S CHILDREN live on the top two floors. Simon and THE FOURTH CHILD live on the first floor. Dry wall and large boards block the doors and halls between the two sections. The Associated Press did not describe the living arrangements of the five Social Services caseworkers who must be assigned to this family around the clock.

I mean, picture this. Here is a family of six, living with a wall separating the two halves of their home. Simon gloats about the fact that when the wall was built, 300 pairs of Chana's shoes were trapped on his side. Chana says that's a lie. Simon says maybe it was only 299; he was just approximating. So help me, if it weren't for the four kids and the homeless shoes, this would be a pretty entertaining affair.

Instead, it swings wildly between Henrik Ibsen and The Three Stooges. It's like watching the Crips and the Bloods fight with Nerf hammers.

You wanna know the best part? These people own another house. TWO DOORS DOWN. Either one of them could have moved into that house three years ago when this all started and they'd be divorced and watching *Lifetime* today. But they'd rather do battle.

---

2   In fairness, I think, had I been her lawyer, I would have advised an appeal, too.

3   They called it "novel." I think the talent of New Yorkers for understatement is perhaps not fully appreciated.

4   "And a peaceful and joyous holiday season to you and yours."

That has caused some to speculate that they might actually still be in love. One therapist was quoted as saying it was clear that if they were willing to go to these lengths, "there's still far too much connection" for a divorce.

Right. This is the kind of thinking that has worked out so well over the years in Bosnia and Kosovo. Tell the Serbs and the Croats and the Bosnians and the Turks there is "too much connection for a divorce."

Or tell it to a jury. That's what the Taubs did. They had a jury trial. Six strangers were chosen by the state of New York to decide whether Mr. and Mrs. Taub could have a divorce. They said no.

NO? THEY SAID NO?! ARE YOU KIDDING ME?!?!

How could they possibly have said no? Did they not know about the wall?

If we were only willing to allow two people on the planet to have a divorce, the Taubs would get my vote. Hell, if we were only willing to allow two people on the planet to have *euthanasia*, they'd get my vote. How could six people not previously identified as serial killers force these two wretches to go on being married?

I don't know. They apparently concluded Mrs. Taub's lamentations about having to flush the toilet after her husband and her complaint that he "made her put on his shoes and socks"[5] did not rise to the level of cruel and inhuman treatment.

Personally, I think the video cameras were the stronger argument. Simon has installed video cameras so he can peer into her side of the house. I might be willing to view that as "cruel and inhuman,"[6] but Chana's argument in that regard was probably weakened by the fact that SHE'S DONE THE SAME THING![7]

Maybe they should have just argued the case differently. Had Chana been my client I would have told the jury, "The synonym for 'inhuman'

---

5   I've quoted this as it appears in the New York Daily News. I'm afraid I cannot tell whether this means he forced her to help him dress or to wear his shoes and socks. Either way, it seems to me that these people are kinda hung up on footwear. Is there such a thing as a shoe/divorce/foot fetish?

6   At least as long as "stupid and creepy" is not grounds for divorce.

7   Sorry about all the caps, but this story seems to me to call for a lot of shouting.

in this context is not 'cruel.' The statute already covers that with the word 'cruel.' So it must be referring to something else when it refers to conduct that is 'inhuman.' In fact, when the statute refers to 'inhuman' conduct, it is referring to conduct that is NON-HUMAN. And since no other humans in the history of the planet have ever conducted themselves like these two, this is clearly NON-HUMAN conduct, even if it isn't cruel."[8]

But that was – sadly – not argued. And, equally sadly, the Taubs remain united in holy deadlock.

So let's recap. We have two people, 57 years old and with all the accumulated wisdom of a fencepost. They have four long-suffering and doubtless psychologically endangered children. After 21 years of marriage, they have descended into a marital maelstrom so grotesque that they have divided their house – and their children – with a wall, on either side of which they have installed video cameras to monitor each other's activities. Their complaints have dwindled to things like, "He doesn't flush the toilet," and "She owns too many shoes." And a jury of six citizens of the great state of New York have decreed that these two people must stay together.

Oyez, Oyez, Oyez! All persons having business before the Honorable, the Supreme Court of the State of New York,[9] are admonished to draw near and give their attention, for the Court is now sitting. God save the State of New York and it's amazing divorce laws.

Can you imagine what this jury trial must have been like? It lasted ten days. Ten days of what Chana's attorney called "a colossal waste of judicial time." All four of the Taubs' children testified for Mom. She said Simon attacked her with everything from a telephone to a treadmill.[10]

---

8   All the presiding judges who did not assign family law cases to me are reading this and nodding sagely.

9   I suppose a good argument can be made that this mess is no more than you can expect from the only place in the world whose trial court is known as the "supreme" court. In New York, you can appeal from the rulings of the Supreme Court to the Court of Appeal. Come to think of it, maybe we should adopt that system here.

10 The kitchen sink was apparently on her side of the wall.

He said he was a pussycat and she was just trying to squeeze cash from a turnip.[11]

And at the end, the jury said no. Somehow Simon's lawyer managed to find the only six strict constructionists in Brooklyn, and they voted to keep the couple "together" – or whatever the correct adverb is for this living arrangement.

So they went home, still married, where – according to Chana – Simon punched her in the eye. Yep. Punched her in the eye.

I will pause here so you can recover from your jaws-agape astonishment and actually close your mouth.

So help me, less than 24 hours after being denied a divorce, they were BOTH back in court: he was claiming she had embarked upon a smear campaign by falsely claiming he hit her, and she was trying to get a judge to look at her shiner. They were both seeking restraining orders in different departments of the same courthouse.

You probably find this case somewhat disturbing, but to me, it's very reassuring. To all those people who didn't think I was smart enough to handle a divorce case, I say, "See, turns out I was EXACTLY smart enough." This is precisely the kind of outcome I would have provided on a daily basis.

---

11 Even the metaphors are scrambled in this case.

"Food Fight!"

"The ideas gained by men before they are twenty-five are practically the only ideas they shall have in their lives."

William James said that, in what was obviously one of his crankier moments. My bet would be that he was at least twice twenty-five when he said it. The simple fact is there are a whole helluva lot more cranky moments after fifty than before.[1]

My own crankiness can be predicted with lunar accuracy. Once a month for the past twenty years, I've faced a deadline for this column.

---

1   Whenever I comment about life after fifty, Justice Sills reminds me to "Wait 'til you hit sixty!" This
    is not helping to make me less cranky.

And, having already stockpiled "practically the only ideas" I shall have in my life before I started writing this drivel, I'm starting to run low and am often hard-pressed to fill this space – wastefully or otherwise.

The problem is compounded by the fact I am a born procrastinator. I live by the adage, "Never put off until tomorrow what – with a little effort – you can delay until a week from Tuesday." So the impending deadline doesn't really show up on my radar until it's too close for missiles or anti-aircraft, and I end up throwing rocks at it – often as it recedes from view.[2]

But almost invariably, often when I'm about to throw in the towel and tell the editor I can't write the column this month because I died, my fellow man[3] provides me with something so surpassingly stupid that it makes me want to apply for membership in some other species. Thoughts like that just have to be exorcised, and I'm grateful to *The Recorder* for allowing me to get them out of my system here rather than in a courtroom or an opinion.

Today's exorcism has to do with interstate commerce, patent law, unfair competition, and peanut butter sandwiches – a conglomeration of ideas rarely juxtaposed as closely or as improbably as they are in this case. All you need to know to realize just how wrong the theory of human evolution is comes from one sentence from today's *Daily Journal.* It says that a company in Orrville, Ohio, "contends it holds the patent for crustless peanut butter and jelly sandwiches and it intends to maintain exclusive rights to the lunchtime staple."

Yep. Patented. Peanut butter and jelly. You got a license? If not, you better get your kids ready for the idea that Mom and Dad are gonna be doing a stretch at Leavenworth, because Menusaver, Inc., is not an outfit to be trifled with.

Just ask Albie's Restaurant. Albie's runs a couple of restaurants in Michigan, and was doubtless more than a little nonplussed to receive

---

2   More than once the editor has called to ask whether I've decided this month to forego the column entirely and just phone the readers personally.

3   I choose this term purposefully: women produce distressingly little grist for my mill. I think they just aren't trying.

a cease-and-desist notice from Menusaver which informed them that Menusaver holds the patent on crustless peanut butter and jelly sandwiches, and would haul Albie's into court to protect that patent. Think about that: a corporation in *another state* sends you a letter saying it has come to their attention that you're selling crustless PBJ's and if you don't cut it out,[4] they're gonna sue your butt.

I'll betcha the first thing the owner of Albie's did was look around the restaurant and try to identify the spy. Who ratted on him? Who told Menusaver he was serving crustless PBJ's?

The second thing had to be this incredible Jim Carry double-take when he realized, "Wait a minute! You can't patent peanut butter and jelly! What are these people smoking?!"

Well, it turns out you *can* patent peanut butter and jelly. I know this because Menusaver did it. In 1999.

NINETEEN NINETY NINE???? NINETEEN NINETY NINE!!!! You mean to tell me if I'd been paying attention in intellectual property class, I coulda patented peanut butter and jelly and never had to meet a deadline in my life? You mean this was just sitting out there unprotected, while moms and dads all over America failed to recognize its potential?

Apparently.

Here's what the patent describes: "The sandwich includes a lower bread portion, an upper bread portion, an upper filling and a lower filling between the lower and upper bread portions, a center filling sealed between the upper and lower fillings and a crimped edge along an outer perimeter of the bread portions for sealing the fillings therebetween."

"Therebetween!" They actually gave a patent to somebody who used the non-word "therebetween." It is inconceivable to me that states disbar lawyers every day but will allow someone who uses the word "therebetween" in a patent application to retain his ticket.

---

4   Or, in this case, stop cutting it off.

And the patent application is for a peanut butter and jelly sandwich![5] It says, "The upper and lower fillings are preferably comprised of peanut butter and the center filling is comprised of at least jelly."[6]

That's it, folks. That's United States Patent No. 6,004,596. Owned by Len C. Kirtchman of Fergus Falls, Minnesota, and David Geske of Fargo, North Dakota. You take two pieces of bread, put peanut butter on each of them, put jelly in the middle, put the bread together so none of the filling is on the outside, and voila! This, the government of the United States of America considers worthy of patent protection.

True, Messrs. Kirtchman and Geske, have come up with the idea of crimping the edges of the bread to keep the filling from falling out. Apparently when the ice fishing in Fergus Falls tapered off, Lenny and Dave sat around playing with their sandwiches and decided crimping was just the thing to make them better. "Hey, Lenny, lookee here what I did. You smash the edges of the sandwich, it gets all doughy and flat, eh? Pretty cool, eh?"

You think this is the idea that impressed the patent examiners? Tell you what. You go home tonight, you make a PBJ. You cut off the crusts. Then you try to crimp the edges to keep the peanut butter and jelly from falling out. Then, after you've cleaned up, you hand the resultant three-bite hors d'ouvre to your six-year-old and see how impressed she is.

But a patent's a patent, I guess, and although this one seems patently absurd, it's gonna take a federal district court to sort it out. That's right. That's how it ended up in the *Daily Journal*. They've made a federal case out of a peanut butter and jelly sandwich.

It's going to be heard on Menusaver's home court – so to speak – the United States District Court in Bay City, Michigan. Way out there

---

5   I'm pretty sure this is the most exclamation points I've ever used in a column. I don't much care for exclamation points, but I can't figure out a way to SHOUT in print.

6   "At least jelly!?" At most, what? Jelly and pate de foie gras? Jelly and motor oil? Jelly and a diamond bracelet?

on the edge of the mitten. Bay City is what would get in your way if you were a moose trying to follow the Saginaw River to Lake Huron.[7]

You wanna know what kinda place Bay City is? Here are the other headlines from the *Bay City Times* the day the PBJ story broke: "Alfalfa Cooperative Files for Bankruptcy," "Au Gres Township Decides to Resurvey for Water Project," and "Councilman Sentenced for Stealing Wallet."[8]

This hardly seems the proper venue for anything as important as PBJ. But, then again, the Scopes Monkey Trial was held in Dayton, Tennessee, and Jack Dempsey fought Fred Werner in Durango, Colorado. At least we don't have to worry about the judge who oversees this awesome conflict doing too much partying. And Dave and Lenny can drive on over from Blizzard Central in their Suburbans, eh?

I figure the rest of us will just teeter on the edge of bankruptcy, waiting to find out if we're gonna owe back royalties to Menusaver. My parents aren't too concerned. Mom always refused absolutely to cut crust off my sandwiches. I don't know whether she was offended by the waste or thought I ought to get used to the cold, hard cruelty of the real world right then and there, but crusts were left on at our house.[9]

But I am a serial crust-nipper. All of my kids, Bill, Megan, and Caitlin, all ate their PBJ's without crusts. Made them happy and gave me a nice little taste of peanut butter and jelly every time I made a sandwich. Seemed like a nice trade-off at the time. Now it means I'm probably gonna have to sign over the 4runner and my hip-waders to Dave and Lenny.

I wonder if they got this idea before they were twenty-five.

---

7   I don't know; why do moose do anything?

8   I oughta move to Bay City; those all sound like columns to me.

9   First they were left on the bread, then they were left on the plate.

"A Criminal Use of Waste"

I don't generally use this space for education. I'm having enough trouble getting myself educated without worrying about others.

But every so often, a case comes along that includes so much wisdom and information that even I – a hopeless Philistine, generally tone-deaf to cultural values – understand immediately that it deserves a wider audience. Such a case is *Navajo Nation v. U. S. Forest Service,* 535 F.3d 1058 (9th Cir. 2008).

I don't know how well you keep up with the advance sheets. I am – sadly – old enough to remember when it was possible to read all the appellate opinions as they were published. Then, as their number grew,

I began concentrating on the criminal ones and skimming the civil. Then I tried to read the "important ones." Now I try to read all the ones written by justices whose names end with "Bedsworth."

But *Navajo Nation* is like a Springsteen Concert or a Rose Parade: even if you're not a fan, *this one* you oughta see. After all, how many cases can be summarized by the *Los Angeles Daily Journal* as, "Government's approval of ski resort to use recycled sewage effluent to make artificial snow on San Francisco Peaks violates Religious Freedom Restoration Act"?

Now isn't that the kinda case you went to law school for? Freedom of religion, recycled sewage effluent, ski resorts, and Native Americans all wrapped up in one case.

Who says the bar exam is unrealistic? You throw in the Rule Against Perpetuities and a testator who has Alzheimer's and speaks only Farsi and you've got next summer's Performance Test, right?

This is a great case, and I'm more than a little jealous. For years, I've kidded my friends on the federal bench[1] that they get the best cases because they somehow got dibs on all the cases that involve treaties and peyote. But a case that involves BOTH!? That's like Lollapalooza 2007. If this case goes to the Supreme Court, they should get Lynyrd Skynyrd to open and provide festival seating for the oral arguments!

Here's what happened: in 1938, developers built a ski resort (Snowbowl) on Humphrey's Peak in the Coconino Mountains of Arizona. Humphrey's is one of four mountains known as the San Francisco Peaks that have "longstanding religious significance to numerous Indian tribes of the American Southwest." In 1938, the idea of building a ski resort on peaks sacred to *another* religion did not offend the people who played golf with legislators, so it got done.

Times change. Now those people – or their heirs – are playing golf at resorts *owned* by Native Americans. And in seventy years, most folks have come around to the conclusion it is difficult to differentiate a ski resort on San Francisco Peaks from a water park at Lourdes or handball

---

1 Actually, the plural here is a little presumptuous. I know one of them is still talking to me, and I think – given enough time – I could think of another somewhere in the system.

courts at the Wailing Wall. So when the ski resort's owners sought to expand their facility, the Forest Service[2] scrutinized the project closely before giving their approval.

At least I *assume* they scrutinized it carefully. I mean, if it had been me, I sure would have been concerned about a plan to spray "treated sewage effluent" that contained "many unidentified and unregulated residual organic contaminants" onto sacred ground.

Actually, I would have been concerned about a plan to spray this stuff on ANY ground. Read that phrase again: "many unidentified and unregulated residual organic contaminants." You know what that is. *The Recorder* would prefer that I not use that particular four-letter word, but when we see phrases like "fecal coliform bacteria" and "detectable levels of enteric bacteria, viruses, and protozoa including Cryptosporidium and Giardia," we grown-ups know what they're talking about, right?

We know what this ... stuff ... is. What we can't figure out is why a *ski resort* would want to make snow out of it.

Didn't we all learn, the first time Mom wrapped us up in thirty pounds of snowsuit and galoshes that outweighed us NOT TO EAT YELLOW SNOW? Wasn't that the first rule of snow play? Forget "sacred ground"; I don't want this stuff on *any ground* where I might do a faceplant.

And if I don't even want to SKI over it, how must the members of the Navajo Nation, the Hopi Tribe, the Havasupai Tribe, the Hualapai Tribe, the Yavapai Apache Nation, and the White Mountain Apache Nation[3] feel about having it sprayed all over their holy place? How would you feel about going for services after "1.5 million gallons a day of treated sewage effluent" had been rained down on your church or synagogue for four months?[4]

---

2   Did I mention that the San Francisco Peaks are federal land? This should eat up another 20 minutes of the poor bar examinees' time.

3   AKA, Plaintiffs.

4   As one Hopi witness put it, "treated sewage effluent is 'something you can't get out of your mind when you're sitting there praying.'" Remind me on Sunday to give thanks that I've never had to try.

Well, it turns out the Forest Service took that into account. So did the ski resort. Turns out they both had lawyers who explained to them both the National Environmental Protection Act (NEPA) and the Religious Freedom Restoration Act (RFRA). The Forest Service and the ski resort considered the advice of their lawyers, but felt they should go ahead with the project because of the "compelling governmental interest" at stake.

Pause for a moment, if you will, to consider that use of the phrase "compelling governmental interest." We're talking about the expansion of a ski resort here. The Forest Service of the United States of America, an agency that has been around for a hundred years and employs thirty-thousand people, thinks expansion of ski resorts is a "compelling governmental interest."[5]

I spent fifteen years as a prosecutor. I am prepared to admit that fifteen years dealing with rape, child molestation, political corruption, and homicide might warp your concept of "compelling governmental interest" a little out of plum, but really ... seriously ..., expansion of a ski resort?

In 2001, there were four skiable days at Snowbowl and 2,857 skiers showed up.[6] By contrast, 13 tribes recognized by the Forest Service consider these mountains sacred and have for centuries. If there's anything compelling about those numbers, it cuts *against* Forest Service approval.[7]

Keep in mind, we're not talking about *eliminating* Snowbowl. The tribes didn't want to *remove* the ski resort. They just didn't want it spraying frozen effluent all over the mountain like some kind of bizarre, mechanical, government-approved cat in heat.

---

5   Yes, this is the same Forest Service that changed Smokey the Bear's name to Smokey Bear and then insisted the rest of us had just hallucinated the middle word all those years.

6   And once word gets out about what they're making snow out of, those 2,857 are gonna drive up the road to Colorado.

7   Compare *Wisconsin v. Yoder* (1972) 406 US 205, 215 ("[O]nly those interests of the highest order and those not otherwise served can overbalance legitimate claims to the free exercise of religion."). Better yet, don't go there; it'll be bad for your blood pressure.

Which brings us back to the National Environmental Protection Act. This is the part of the case that has always commanded my attention. I belong to a religion that believes flaming shrubberies can talk and that the minimum number of animals necessary to propagate a species is one male, one female, and one ark. So it can probably be convincingly argued that I have a tin ear when it comes to religious arguments.[8]

But I can hear the environment just fine. And turning a ski slope into Yellowacre ... well, that gets my attention. And it got the 9th Circuit's attention. As an appellate judge, I can tell you that anytime you find yourself beginning a section of your opinion with the heading, "Human Ingestion of Snow Made from Treated Sewage Effluent," you are going to be completely focused. At least you are if you have skiers in your family.

The problem was complicated by the fact that the State of Arizona had somehow concluded that frozen sewage effluent was perfectly okay as artificial snow but wholly unacceptable for human ingestion. I can only conclude these people have never skied, because these two conclusions are incompatible.

If it can't be swallowed, it can't be skied upon. When you're rolling ass over teakettle through snow, wondering how you lost your edge, listening for the telltale sound of bones breaking or ligaments snapping, you will not be able to control what goes into your mouth, any more than you can control what comes out of it.

But the Forest Service and the ski resort owners insisted that this particular sewage had been approved for use as artificial snow by the State of Arizona, so how bad could it be? How to deal with the "no ingestion" component of that approval seemed to them a question for another day.[9]

But in fact, as the 9th Circuit concluded, that is a question that requires an answer *before* the first-day skiers hit the saffron Snowbowl

---

8   Although I can apparently detect a few more notes than the U.S. Forest Service.

9   As I recall, they suggested April 27, 2093.

slopes. As the Havasupai pointed out, that's when "[k]ids and skiers will be getting a mouthful of [the water]."

That last phrase is a quote from the opinion. I love the fact the 9th Circuit chose to bowdlerize the Havasupai argument. Without access to the Havasupai brief, we will never know what word or phrase the euphemistic "[the water]" stands for.[10]

But whatever words the Havasupai used, they were good enough to convince the 9th Circuit that the Forest Service and the developer had managed to violate both RFRA and NEPA in one fell[11] swoop. Essentially, they said, "You didn't think about this nearly hard enough. Go back and try it again. Better yet, *don't* try this again. Ever."

That concludes the educational component of today's program. We hope you've learned not to urinate on other people's property and not to eat yellow snow. If you have, you are probably no further along than you were when you were eleven, but you are ahead of the United States Forest Service, and that's a start.

---

10 I have two guesses, both involving four letters, both words *The Recorder* would rather I not use.

11 VERY fell.

Hysteropotmoi. Honest.

This one you aren't gonna believe. Hell, you probably think I make most of this stuff up anyway, so I suppose it's redundant to warn you that more credibility-flogging is on the way. But this one's a beaut.

I had to look up the phrase "hypothetical yearly tenancy" the other day. Now right away you know this Court of Appeal gig is not all it's cracked up to be. Jobs that require you to sweep out the stables or say no to rock stars or get bitten by spiders regularly might still be good jobs. A job that requires you to look up "hypothetical yearly tenancy" cannot possibly pay enough.

I tried to avoid looking the phrase up. First, I tried to figure it out using nothing more authoritative than my own mind.[1]

I mean, these were three words with which I was reasonably conversant. They weren't especially difficult words, and I had used each of them regularly throughout my career. But try as I might, I couldn't begin to figure out what their juxtaposition could signify.

It was as if I'd been going through a cookbook and came across the phrase "oyster crockpot sommelier." I knew what the words meant; I just couldn't put them together and get anything but dissonance.

But a federal circuit court had made sense of them in a case I needed to understand, so I had to somehow mold them into a form which was recognizable in my cosmos. I gave it my best shot.

"Hypothetical yearly tenancy." Alright, this is where you theorize about what life would be like if you lived for a year in a rented condo in Boise.

No? Okay, it's when you call an expert to assume the existence of a one-year lease and then ask him inane questions about it.

No? Then it's pretending the year only has five months because you're living on Mercury. (I thought this one had promise, since federal circuit judges are almost certainly extraterrestrial and might therefore have occasion for hypothetical extraterrestrial year calculations, but it just didn't fit in the context of the case.)

I finally had to make two unhappy admissions. First, I had not the slightest idea what the phrase meant. And second, I had no law clerk who'd transgressed in any way which would justify saddling him with it. I had to look it up myself.

So I pulled my Black's off the shelf, shoveled six cubic yards of dust off it, and paged halfway into the longest plotless work ever written by someone not named Michener. Sure enough, there it was: hypothetical yearly tenancy, "The basis, in England, of rating lands and hereditaments to the poor-rate, and to other rates and taxes that are expressed to be leviable or assessable in like manner as the poor-rate."

---

1   And you don't get a whole lot less authoritative than that.

Say what?

Now I *was* confused. I closed the book and looked at the cover to make sure I had not picked up Black's English-To-Some-Other-Language-You've-Never-Previously-Encountered Dictionary.

"Rating lands and hereditaments to the poor rate?" "Expressed to be leviable or assessable in like manner?" Who wrote this, Chewbacca the Wookie? You could hold a Sanskrit computer program up to a mirror and read every third word and it would make more sense than this.

These were most definitely words I was *not* reasonably conversant with.[2] Nor was my spell-check program. My page as I type this is covered with little red worms under questionable words. It looks like a manuscript viewed through the eyes of Keith Richards after a Stones concert.

Go ahead. Read it again. Is this, or is it not, the legal equivalent of "Fold Flap A across Tab 3 and staple both to opposite ends of the appropriate snipe flanges." This has to be the same guy who ghost-wrote *Daubert v. Merrill-Dow Pharmaceuticals.* I thought Casey Stengel was dead.

I read it a half-dozen times and then just started laughing. This has to be somebody's idea of a joke. Somebody at the Black's Law Dictionary Company won a bet on this one. I figure when this edition was published, one of the researchers turned to the guy in the next cubicle and said, "Pay me, Antonin; I told you the editors never read what we write."

And Antonin, cursing softly as he handed over the twenty, grumbled, "Fluke. Just a gawddammed fluke. You couldn't do it again if your life depended on it."

"Do it again?" Abelard the Wordsmith roared, "I could do it fifty times. I've already convinced 'em that "hwata" or "hwatung" means, "In old English law. Augury; divination." I've already gotten 'em to publish "Hypobolum" with the explanation that it was "the name of the

---

2   Although I have now renamed my fantasy baseball team the "Laguna Beach Hereditaments."

bequest or legacy given by the husband to his wife, at his death, above her dowry."

"'Hwatung' and 'hypobolum,' Antonin. You know how I got 'hwatung?' I banged all my fingers down on the keyboard at once and held them there for a count of three. My fingers made that word up."

"If they believed those, they'll believe anything. In fact, I don't think we *have* editors anymore. I think whatever we write just goes to the janitor and he gets paid an extra fifty dollars a month for alphabetizing 'em."

And Antonin, loyal company man that he was,[3] said, "I got another twenty says you can't do it again."

So Abelard, envisioning another night of Guinness instead of Budweiser, threw back his head in laughter and said, "Make it $40 and I'll do it *on the same page*! I'll make up a word nobody could ever, not for a New York minute, think was a real word. And then I'll make up a definition – the dumbest, most unbelievable, most palpably laughable definition since the Scots invented curling[4] – and I'll put the dumb made-up word and the even dumber made-up definition on the same page as the 'hypothetical yearly tenancy' and our editors will swallow it hook, line, sinker, rod, reel, bass boat, and Chevy Suburban. You just watch."

And that, boys and girls, has to be how the word, "hysteropotmoi" made it into the Fifth Edition of Black's Law Dictionary.

Yep, there it is. Just one word away from "hypothetical yearly tenancy." The word that cost poor, loyal, straight-arrow Antonin forty bucks because the idiot editors left it in. Right there on page 743 of Black's Law Dictionary: hysteropotmoi.

Is that a real word? Oh, absolutely. I'm sure of it. Let's see, "hystero" from the Greek *hysterikos*, indicating a delusion. And "pot" from the

---

3   But admittedly shaken to realize that "hwatung" was in Black's as an old English word rather than a province in China.

4   A game in which rocks with handles on them (yes, handles) are pushed across an ice surface toward a shuffleboard goal while players try to adjust their course (the rocks' course, not the players') by melting the ice by sweeping it with brooms so fast that friction melts it. Honest. This one's not in Black's Law Dictionary, it's on Canadian television, so I'm pretty sure it exists.

Latin *potare*, meaning "to drink." And *moi* from the French word for "me."

So "hysteropotmoi" would be a delusionary state in which the sufferer believes others are trying to drink her. Of course. Actually, that was a lot easier than the "hypothetical yearly tenancy" thing.

But that's not the definition Black's has. Oh no. You wanna know what Black's says? You wanna know what Abelard actually got the editors of Black's Law Dictionary to sign off on? Alright, here it is:

"Those who, having been thought dead, had, after a long absence in foreign countries, returned safely home; or those who, having been thought dead in battle, had afterwards unexpectedly escaped from their enemies and returned home. These, among the Romans, were not permitted to enter their own houses at the door, but were received at a passage opened in the roof."

"A passage opened in the roof?" "A passage opened in the roof?!" Oh sure. I can picture this without a whole lot of trouble. Guy comes home from five years of battling Ostrogoths and his wife greets him at the door and says, "Gee, Hon,[5] you've been gone so long, we thought you were dead. I'm afraid I'm remarried to Fergie the Langobard. You'll have to enter through a hole in the roof until we get this all sorted out." Oh, hell yeah, probably happened all the time.

How could they print that? How could anybody think that was a real word? What was going on in their brapscraggins?[6]

As you can tell, I'm pretty upset about this whole thing. I mean, I expect basketball players and anchorwomen and sword-swallowers to have more fun than I do, but philologists?!

There's a lot more I could say about this, but I don't have the time. I gotta go work on my car. Johnson rod broke yesterday and sheared a Knudsen nut right off. I'll be working on it all day. You wouldn't know anybody who has a set of metric Trahorn wrenches would you?

---

5   Or, "Hun," as the case may be.

6   A word which would have been in the next edition of Black's if Abelard hadn't tired of this game and taken a job in advertising.

Eat, Drink, and Hire Lawyers

The Apocalypse is nigh.

I know this because the Bible says so. "War, famine, pestilence, and Major League Eating." I'm pretty sure those are the four horsemen John the Divine partied with on Patmos while penning the Book of Revelation.

And sure enough, two thousand years later, Joey Chestnut has introduced the End of Days by eating 50 hot dogs in ten minutes.

I know this because I read it on the ESPN ribbon on the bottom of my TV screen while I was watching a baseball game. We got a big screen a few years back so I could read the ribbon from my favorite chair fifteen feet away. So far this is the most disturbing thing I've read.

The ribbon went on to explain that Chestnut had accomplished this amazing feat without the distraction of competition from Tareku Kobayashi, who had been barred from the competition *because he refused to sign a contract with Major League Eating.*

Honest, that's what it said. It said there is something called Major League Eating. And they have contracts.

As near as I can determine, this entity sponsors contests in which people vie to force comestibles into their bodies faster than anyone else can.

Of course, if you've ever watched one of these contests, you know they have nothing to do with eating. This isn't eating, any more than using a chainsaw to demolish a guitar is music.

The contestants splash hot dogs (complete with buns) into bowls of water to soften them and then stuff them down their esophagi for ten minutes, not so much chewing as vacuuming. If this is eating, why is it no one else on the planet soaks their hot dogs in water before eating them plain ... and wet?

Is it just me, or is this the kind of wretched excess that brought down the Roman Empire, the Etruscan civilization, and the Three Tenors? Seriously, how many steps are there between paying money to watch people force bratwurst down their alimentary canals and paying money to watch lions force Christians down their alimentary canals?

Fifty apple fritters in 10 minutes? That's eating. Fifty dim sum? Sure. Been there.

But fifty things you couldn't eat one of without bringing up last night's lasagna? That's not eating, that's water-boarding with Oscar Mayer.

And yet Major League Eating[1] must be a serious enterprise. They have a logo and a website – which is about all it takes these days to

---

1   Not to be confused with Major League Baseball, whose grip on reality is only slightly less tenuous, but who at least knows how to eat a hot dog.

convince people you're respectable – and a commissioner and a Hall of Fame.

Oops, check that; the website says the Hall of Fame is "coming soon." So I may have jumped the gun there.

But their headquarters is in New York, where all serious people live. That should make up for the not-ready-for-prime-time Hall of Fame.

The website is the key to legitimacy. We've now raised a couple of generations of people who believe anything they read on the Internet. These people believe the government has been lying to them ever since Roswell. They think the "mainstream press" is engaged in some kind of vast, anti-competitive conspiracy to suppress "the truth."

But they will believe Elvis Presley is alive and living in an abandoned Burger King in Tulsa, if they get an email from an uncredentialed stranger that says so.

I know this because they forward these emails to me daily. And if I have the temerity to challenge them, I'm immediately referred to ElvisIsAlive.com or WhyWon'tObamaAdmitHeCamefromPluto.com, as if that pretty much settles that.

For these people, having a website proves that Major League Eating is a real sport. And having both a website and a logo just like the NBA and the NFL and NASCAR – well that eliminates any doubt about the organization's bona fides.

That's probably why they have recognition by ESPN. ESPN generally sets the bar low enough that it's indistinguishable from a speed bump. This is, after all, a network that got its start televising Australian Rules Football and dressage.

You got a website AND a logo? You're in. Welcome to ESPN coverage.

And for a fledgling sports[2] league, recognition by ESPN is pretty much what recognition by the UN would be to a group of rebels living in corrugated tin lean-tos in the jungle and tossing hand grenades at passing soldiers.

---

[2]   Jeez, it hurts me to apply that word to this activity.

Once ESPN puts you into the ribbon, you're the real deal. You've arrived. You can start negotiating sponsorship deals with people other than the hot dog company and Pepto Bismol.[3]

And, of course none of this can be accomplished without the invaluable[4] assistance of our profession. MLE seems to have recognized this need. After all, the ESPN ribbon said that Mr. Kobayashi had not been allowed to compete in the annual Fourth of July Coney Island Fiascorama Face Stuffing[5] because he had not signed a contract with MLE.[6] So it appears they are all lawyered up and ready to go.

Which is good. Because you don't have to watch a competitive eating match for long before you absolutely KNOW these people are using performance-enhancing drugs. I mean, how many roofies would it take before you would soak a hot dog and bun in water and eat it? What kind of hallucinogenic would you need to stuff these concoctions down your gullet fifty times in 10 minutes?

So they will inevitably need Roger Clemens' and Barry Bonds' and Marian Jones' lawyers for their players. And the Justice Department will, of course, need to employ additional staff to mis-try the cases against the MLE Hall of Famers.[7]

There will be more work for criminal lawyers as competitive gourmands develop the athletic sense of entitlement that seems inevitably to show up in bars, nightclubs, and drunk-driving arraignment courts around the country. And the same competitors will need lawyers to negotiate their endorsement contracts as the youth of America scramble to make sure they're using the same antacids as their heroes.

---

3 Really. Near as I can determine, MLE's sponsors are Nathan's hot dogs and Pepto Bismol. I guess you gotta play the cards you're dealt.

4 And yet high-priced.

5 Or whatever it was called.

6 I must admit to a certain bemusement here. While the logo of Major League Eating consists of a left hand thrusting a fork in front of the letters MLE, the official website lists the organization's name as the International Federation of Competitive Eating, Inc. (More proof they have lawyers.)

7 Once they get a Hall of Fame.

We'll need labor lawyers to handle the strikes and lockouts. The NBA and NFL folks should bring a ton of experience[8] to those tables.

There will be leagues. There will be franchises. Lots of work for corporate types. Copyright lawyers will have to study the team names and logos. And, of course, there will be work for bankruptcy lawyers and divorce lawyers if the league lets out a franchise in Los Angeles.

Antitrust lawyers will have to see about getting an exemption like MLB's for MLE.

Wrongful death specialists will be called in to handle the cases of the survivors of twelve-year-olds who think this is their future. "I remember just last Christmas, we gave him ten packages of Dodger dogs and sixty buns and a Joey Chestnut autographed water dish. He was so happy. And now he's gone. It's all their fault."

And while there's really no telling where all this will end, we can be pretty sure that no good can come from anything that starts with soaking hot dogs in water. And wherever there is "no good" you need lawyers.

All in all, probably not a favorable development for civilization.

But for a legal profession hit hard by recession? A bonanza.

God bless MLE and the International Federation of Competitive Eating, Inc. Now can someone direct me to the offices of the International Federation of Competitive Choking and Gagging, Inc. I hear they might need a goal judge.

---

8   And a ton of money.

Bureaucrats 1, Rocket Scientists 0

I was a prosecutor for 15 years at the beginning of my career. It was tougher then. Writing hadn't yet been invented, and we had all those pesky dinosaurs to deal with.

My early mentors were less concerned with my appreciation of the music of the spheres than they were with my development of perspective. Maybe it was just because they figured I needed help with the basics more than my peers, but the lessons I was taught as a tyro prosecutor had a lot more to do with human beings – the care and handling of judges, jurors, court staff, victims, witnesses and the defense bar – than they did with *People v. Gazorninplat* and whether a warrant was required to open a locked box in the trunk of a car that had been torched in a private parking garage that had subsequently collapsed in an earthquake in which the car's owner was killed.

They pretty much assumed I'd learned enough law in Berkeley to be able to try someone for disturbing the peace without bringing the American judicial system and the entire common law tradition crashing down around my ears. But they weren't sure I yet knew how to interview a rape victim or identify with a 40-year-old career motorcycle officer. They were right, of course – at least about the last part.

The late Al Wells, a legendary Orange County prosecutor, once told me, "We don't need the smartest guys in the class to do this job. We don't need the law review types and the coifs. We don't need rocket scientists. We need people with good judgment."

I was 24 years old. I was so wet behind the ears you could have grown rice on my neck. "Al," I asked him, "how do you get good judgment?"

And Al, who'd been a prosecutor since Caesar was a border guard, flashed that warm, avuncular smile and said, "By exercising bad judgment, Billy; that's why God made misdemeanors."

So we greenhorns all learned the rules of evidence and the complexities of human nature by trying misdemeanors. If you dropped the blood vial in a driving-under-the-influence case and watched it shatter on the floor – as actually happened to one of my contemporaries – you were not turning a puppy-raper loose on society. If you over-prosecuted a petty theft case, it was unlikely your mistake would change the earth's rotational rate.

The idea was that you would do stupid things early in your career and learn from them how not to do stupid things later in your career. With that in mind, I find myself wondering who handled the NCAA's investigation of Cal Tech.

That's right. The NCAA went after Cal Tech.

Using Al Wells' logic, I figure their case was handled by the last guy in the door. I figure it has to be the last person they hired to perform duties that do not routinely involve a bucket and a mop.

For those of you not numbered among the sporting cognoscenti, let me identify the parties here. The NCAA is the National Collegiate Athletic Association – the agency putatively responsible for managing college athletics.[1] In the drama I am about to describe to you, they will be played by Goliath.

Cal Tech is the California Institute of Technology. Cal Tech, along with MIT, is the premier scientific learning institution in America. This is where you go if you're too smart for Harvard and Yale and Cal and Stanford. This is where Al Wells would have looked for rocket scientists if he had decided he needed them.

But as stellar as Cal Tech's intellectual firepower is, their athletic record is ... well, what's the opposite of stellar? Troglodytic? Subterranean? God bless 'em, the Beavers[2] have raised losing to an art form. In today's performance, they will be played not by David, but by David's third understudy's accountant.

How bad are the Beavs? Their baseball team has lost 237 straight games. 237 STRAIGHT. These guys are more likely to find the Higgs Boson than home plate.

I played on some pretty bad baseball teams in my day. I didn't stop playing until I reached law school,[3] and the fact these teams included me on their roster was a pretty good indicator they were familiar with a level of desperation not encountered by too many athletic programs. I played on teams so bad we didn't need a bus; the other team sent limos to pick us up.

I experienced losing. I experienced losing streaks. But I never imagined it was even *possible* to lose 237 in a row. Seems like you'd win one or two *by mistake.*

But at Cal Tech, it's not only possible, it's something of a tradition. The water polo team once went nine years without a win. The

---

1   I use the word "putatively" here because we all know the NCAA's control over college athletics is a fiction. Television and Nike manage college athletics. Everyone else is irrelevant.

2   Yep. Cal Tech Beavers.

3   Actually, not even then, but that's another embarrassing story, and I only have room for the one today.

basketball team went 310 consecutive games without a win, a 26-year streak that began in the mid-eighties and ended in 2011 with a one-point victory over Occidental.

Which I think is both more remarkable and more admirable than any of the trophy-laden records posted by the schools we watch on national television every week. It's college sport, for crying out loud. It should be about competing and having fun and building character – not grooming professional athletes.

Given my choice of having a beer with the quarterback of last year's national championship football team or having one with the coach of a team that hasn't won in a half-dozen years, I'll pick the latter every time.

But the NCAA apparently has rookies in its enforcement department, just as Al Wells had them in the D. A.'s Office, and needs misdemeanors for them to practice on. So it has announced sanctions against Cal Tech.

Sanctions!

Really? These people win every time Halley's Comet comes around and you're gonna sanction them? What in the world can you do to them?

Actually, how to sanction a school like Cal Tech is a problem. When USC, a perennial sports powerhouse, was sanctioned a few years back, the NCAA took away some scholarships and banned them from post-season play.

Cal Tech has no athletic scholarships, and the only way they're going to see post-season play is on their television sets – which the students build themselves.

Nonetheless, the NCAA has banned them from post-season play in 2013. This level of cerebration indicates to me that if they'd had jurisdiction, the NCAA would have banned Adam Sandler from Academy Award consideration, Richard Simmons from the Olympic Games, and me from appointment to The Hague.

This is precisely the kind of rookie judgment call Al Wells had in mind for young prosecutors. Those of you with young associates might want to consider farming them out to the NCAA for a year.

And what was the transgression that brought down the Battlin' Beavs?[4] What was the crime that will end their dream of a Sugar Bowl appearance next season or a trip to The Final Four? What was the rule that eluded these people who have so completely mastered the arcane and esoteric[5] laws of physics?

Well, it seems Cal Tech students are allowed to sit in on classes for three weeks at the start of each term to help them decide which ones to take. If the class looks good, they sign up; if not, they take something else. Makes sense to me. And it means they're gonna know three weeks more about something than they would have otherwise because they needed that time to decide not to take the class.

Brilliant! They've found a way to get students to take EXTRA classes!

But in the eyes of the NCAA, that's a no-no. According to the NCAA, they aren't students for those three weeks. *They haven't signed up for courses.* If you haven't signed up for courses, you're not a student. So all this time, Cal Tech has been going o for forever WITH RINGERS!

So whoever occupies the lowest rung on the NCAA ladder decided Cal Tech needed to be punished for letting that academic decision cloud their athletic judgment. They are now officially on NCAA probation. Right along with the big boys: Alabama, Boise State, USC, Penn State, and most colleges in Florida.

Thank you, NCAA. It's been a long time since I got to hear Al Wells' laugh. And now I can hear it quite clearly.

---

4   No, as far as I know, no one calls them that but me.

5   Not to say nonsensical. So help me, the more I read about string theory and multi-dimensional physics, the more convinced I am these guys are just making stuff up.

BEDS NOTES

1. I use the word "putatively" here because we all know the NCAA's control over college athletics is a fiction. Television and Nike manage college athletics. Everyone else is irrelevant.

2. Yep. Cal Tech Beavers.

3. Actually, not even then, but that's another embarrassing story, and I only have room for the one today.

4. Sorry, Dick Luesebrink and other Oxy Tigers; I didn't think I could leave that fact out.

5. No, as far as I know, no one calls them that but me.

6. Not to say nonsensical. So help me, the more I read about string theory and multi-dimensional physics, the more convinced I am these guys are just making stuff up.

Is That a Kielbasa in Your Pocket?

It occurred to me today that it's a long, long time from May to December, but the days grow short when you reach September.[1] Which means that by October, the days have grown short enough that Grumpy and Sneezy could drive the lane on them. The race to get home before sunset has once again become an even-money proposition, and the smart money's on the sun.

---

1   Of course, it occurred to Kurt Weill fifty years ago, when he wrote *September Song*. But don't go thinking there's nothing new in the world until you've read a little further.

All of which means another year has slipped by us[2] without a major weight loss or a personal best time or an organized garage or a last will and testament. How does this happen every year?

God, in Her wisdom, has seen to it that the Yankees still haven't won a pennant in the 21st century, so we know that there are some fronts on which the forces of evil and sloth have been reduced to a holding action. But a year that winds down with the Secretary of the Treasury holding a gun to the economy and saying, "Give me $700 billion dollars in unmarked bills or Wall Street dies," is not one you're gonna want to paste into your memory book next to the senior prom.

So I am especially pleased to brighten your skies with the announcement of the winner of this year's annual Jimmy Dean Best Crime Committed with a Sausage Award.

Some of you may have noticed that the annual Jimmy Dean Best Crime Committed with a Sausage Award has been something less than strictly annual of late. Sausage crime seems to have fallen off now that the Department of Homeland Security has put sausages on its list of dangerous terrorist devices, along with the eyeglass cleaning solution I was required to discard before my last flight.[3]

So you can imagine how pleased I was when loyal reader Jeff Williams of Schiff Hardin in San Francisco[4] sent me the article describing this year's award-winning entry. The article is from the *Fresno Bee*.[5] It begins, "A burglar who broke into a home just east of Fresno rubbed food seasoning over the body of one of two men as they slept in their rooms and then used an 8-inch sausage to whack the other man on the face and head before running out of the house, Fresno county sheriff's deputies said Saturday."

---

2   Let's face it, between Halloween, Thanksgiving, December holidays, and the week-long bacchanalia that is my birthday, nothing much gets done after mid-October.

3   Hard to argue with that logic: Terrorists who can read the in-flight magazine are indubitably more dangerous than terrorists who can't.

4   That's Jeff right over there, jumping off the roof over having been outed as 1/5 of my readership.

5   Come to think of it, maybe Jeff jumped off the roof over being outed as a reader of the *Fresno Bee*. That would be hard for someone living in San Francisco to explain.

Wow. Breathtaking, isn't it. Read that over again and you'll begin to understand why sausage crimes get their very own award.

Food seasoning. He rubbed "Pappy's Seasoning" – a local product, highly prized in Fresno epicurean circles – on the body of a sleeping man. Why would anybody want to do that? And why would they want to do it so much they would break into a home in the dead of night to accomplish it?[6]

Unfortunately, the *Bee*'s article does not identify WHICH "Pappy's Seasoning" was used. Obviously, the intent of the burglar is much more difficult to divine without knowing whether he used "Pappy's Choice Seasoning," "Pappy's Louisiana Hot Spice," or "Pappy's Prime Rib Rub," and I would have expected a fine paper like the *Bee* to have been more specific. But, as you can imagine, police are often very tight-lipped about details with sausage crime, for fear of inspiring copycat crimes, so the dearth of information on this point may have reflected official law enforcement policy as much as reportorial indolence.

As is often the case with sausage crime, the intent is largely inferable from the suspect's attire. In this case, the suspect, one Antonio Vasquez Jr., 21, of Fresno, "ran out of the house wearing only a t-shirt, boxer shorts and socks, leaving behind his wallet with his ID." Why are we not surprised by this news?

This tells us a couple of rather disturbing things. But before we get to them, let's pause for a moment to contemplate once again the unimaginably strange life of a peace officer. These poor cops were summoned to a nighttime "burglary in progress call," a serious felony that can be expected to both wake up your adrenal glands and unfasten the strap on your holster at pretty much the same time. So after preparing to confront Charles Manson, bloody knife in hand, they instead ended up arresting a nearly naked guy who had slathered seasoning rub on one sleeping victim and then whacked the other with a tube of meat. How do you survive roller coaster rides like that with even a tenuous grip on sanity?

---

6   Especially since you can only rub meat seasoning on a sleeping man for a very short time before he ceases to be a sleeping man and becomes a very awake man. I would imagine.

Alright, now that we've had a moment to thank the Lord that our son or daughter didn't go into a field as mental-health-threatening as law enforcement, let's get back to the couple of rather disturbing things I mentioned at the start of the last paragraph. Try to keep up, here. I don't have time to re-write these things into a cohesive structure with linear trains of thought. I have a day job.

First, of course, the leaving behind the wallet thing is an obvious cry for help. It would be difficult to say, "Stop me before I rub seasoning on people and hit them with a sausage again," more clearly. In fact, if you just ask yourself how many times in your life you've heard someone say, "Stop me before I rub seasoning on people and hit them with a sausage again," you will realize how difficult it must be to say that *at all*, much less clearly. So leaving behind your ID is probably the best way to do it.[7]

Second, it tells us the burglar apparently disrobed partially before beginning his nefarious seasoning and sausage-wielding activities.[8] To a trained student of the criminal psyche, this speaks volumes. The difference in culpability between a fully-clothed sausage-wielding seasoning-rubber and a boxer-clad t-shirt-wearing sausage-wielding seasoning-rubber is ... well ... huge.

Which, of course, brings us to the sausage. The eight-inch sausage.[9] To me, the sausage is the key to the case.

Let me explain. Antonio Vasquez allegedly[10] broke into the home of two farmworkers outside Fresno, stripped to his underwear, and then began rubbing one of the men with Pappy's Seasoning and beating the other with a sausage. The men awoke, Antonio boogied, and he was

---

7   It is not, for example, something you can say with flowers. Or fruit. And, as near as I can determine, Hallmark hasn't even tried.

8   My original draft said "sausage-battering" but that sounded way too culinary, somehow. It seemed to me to suggest he was getting ready to deep-fry the sausage, which may have been the case, but has not yet been charged.

9   Insert your own tasteless joke here. My editor vetoed the three I came up with.

10   "Allegedly" is, of course, a crucial word here. When you accuse someone of something as serious as sausage crime, you have to be careful to remind readers that he is not a sausage-wielding, seasoning-rubbing weirdo until it is proven beyond a reasonable doubt.

apprehended in a nearby field in his underwear. His ID was found at the scene, along with his pants, and he was found – sans pants – cowering in a nearby field. So this is not exactly a whodunit.

Intent will be the issue here. Under California law, burglary is the entry of a building *with the intent to commit a theft or a felony*. If you don't have one of those intents, you aren't a burglar. So if Antonio didn't take anything, he may be able to beat the rap, if the prosecution cannot show he intended to commit a felony.

I was a prosecutor for 15 years. I can imagine the consternation generated in the D.A.'s Office by the collective effort to figure out what felony Antonio might have had in mind. I'm sure their Sausage Crimes Task Force has been burning the midnight oil trying to find a felony that fits these facts. "Let's see, what crime involves rubbing meat seasoning on your victim? Uh, well that would be ... um ... uh ... that would be ... um .... Well, wait a minute; the guy was half-naked. Obviously, his intent with the seasoning was to ... to ... uh .... Um, the sausage; don't forget the sausage. Clearly, he was going to commit the crime of ... the crime of .... Aw, sh_t, it's gotta be *something*!"

Hence, the importance of the sausage. Assault with a deadly weapon or assault by means of force likely to produce great bodily harm would be felonies. Those are general intent crimes that wouldn't require six Freudians and a cultural anthropologist to sell to a jury. So how big and hard was the sausage? Is it the type of weapon you would expect to do serious harm to someone if used as a cudgel?

This question was directed to Lieutenant Ian Burrimond of the Fresno Sheriff's Department. Lieutenant Burrimond – a man who must have done something VERY bad in his last life to get stuck with this case – was forced to look right into the camera and say that – unfortunately – the sausage was discarded by the suspect as he fled ... and ... wait for it ... wait for it ... EATEN BY THE VICTIMS' DOG!

That's right. In the immortal words of Lieutenant Burrimond, "The dog ate the weapon."

This is, of course, not the best defense ever devised. Any kid who ever tried to explain his failure to produce a homework assignment with the claim that it was eaten by the family dog can attest to the general ineffectiveness of this strategy.

But it's better than nothing. Those dog-slandering kids didn't have Lieutenant Burrimond on their witness list. What's more, they had the burden of proof. Antonio Velasquez doesn't. He can just sit back and watch the prosecutor herniate trying to push that reasonable doubt boulder up the mountain. He's got at least as good a shot as Ernesto Miranda, and we all know how that turned out.[11]

So let's hear it for Antonio. Not only did he win this year's Jimmy Dean Award, he came up with the groundwork for the perfect burglary. Henceforth, anyone contemplating a res burg would be well-advised to take with him an 8-inch sausage and a jar of meat seasoning. Then, if your intended victims awaken or come home, strip to your underwear and start rubbing them with the seasoning, whack 'em with the sausage a coupla times, bark like a dog, and break for the door.[12]

Worst case scenario is misdemeanor time. You can do that standing on your head. And if you're as goofy as Antonio Velasquez, that's probably exactly how you'll choose to do it.

---

11 *Miranda v. Arizona* (1966) 384 U. S. 436.

12 The dog barking thing is my own idea. I think a good Velasquez Defense just cries out for an insanity plea.

The Bridge

I've been writing this column for 32 years. In all that time, nearly four hundred columns, I can count on one hand the number of times I've gotten serious with you. Brace yourself: this will be one of those times.

If you came here looking for a laugh – and were desperate enough to turn to me –you might as well stop reading right here and turn the page. Get hold of a copy of the Congressional Record. That should make you laugh – at least until you start weeping.

But it says at the bottom of every column that I write it to get it out of my system, and that is literally true. I'm a guy who needs to laugh, and I've spent my life in jobs – prosecutor, judge, justice – that don't involve much laughter.

Everything I write in my day job makes somebody unhappy. And no one wants to read, "Your five million dollar judgment is reversed, but did you hear the one about the nun and the parrot and the sailor?"

So usually the column allows me to get my laugh fix without doing it at the expense of others.[1] Unfortunately, this month I have something else to get out of my system.

My best friend died. Last night.

His name was Tom Wilkinson. He went by "Wilk" most of his life. In college, where he set a school record for fielding percentage, his teammates changed that to "Silk," as in "smooth as ..." and I called him that the rest of his life.

We met in the 5th grade. His mom had fled the poverty of South Central Los Angeles for our blue-collar neighborhood a couple miles away, where nobody was rich, but everybody qualified for a home loan under the GI Bill.

His mom was a waitress, my dad was a casketmaker; I thought we were "upper-middle-class." He knew better. And he spent the rest of his life giving me reality checks.

In 56 years, we never had a serious falling-out. We did everything together. We played Little League together, we trick-or-treated together, we struggled through puberty together. We studied for the SAT together, played college ball together, got Christmas vacation and summer jobs together. We were each other's best man. I have very few memories of my life that Silk didn't celebrate or suffer through with me.

Cancer took him out. Like me, he was barely 66.

I'm writing this to share with you something he said to me when he first learned of his cancer. I have shared it with others, but this platform gives me a chance to share it with people who don't know me – people in Atlanta and St. Louis and Washington, D. C., and all the other places

---

1   Well, no others except my readers.

that run my column. I think it's something everyone –especially every lawyer – should hear.

Silk was a smoker. He quit after 30 years, but the damage had already been done. His cancer was smoking-related.

When he found that out, he recalled all the times he'd said, "We'll cross that bridge when we get to it." That was his mantra for all the years he smoked. That was what he said to all the well-meaning people who tried to get him to stop.

And when they diagnosed his problem, he said to me, "You feel pretty stupid when you actually get to the goddam bridge."

Silk got to the bridge in his fifties. He spent the rest of his life trying to cross it while battling not just the disease, but the poisons of chemo-therapy, the burns of radiation, and the suppurating wounds of surger-ies in places you wouldn't even want a bruise.

It turned his life from the triumphal march of a collegiate star athlete, successful businessman ("Plastics, my boy, plastics."), loving husband, and proud father, to the dogged trudge of a stoic but badly damaged infantryman. It was a bridge too far.

He never once complained about this, never questioned its fairness, never whined or griped or sank into self-pity. He understood com-pletely that actions have consequences, and he considered his plight a simple matter of cause-and-effect. He took it better than I did.

In the end, he chose hospice care rather than extending his life with more chemo, and his only comment about hospice care was how great the people were and how hard they tried to make him comfortable. In the last months of his life, I only heard him verbalize two feelings: gratitude and pain.

We went to one last baseball game together three months ago in Atlanta. We had seats we would have dreamed about as kids, but he was taking a lot of pain medication, twisting in his hard plastic seat, and it was the first time I ever saw him turn down a ballpark hot dog.

On the other side of me sat a man who had driven in from South Carolina to bring his boy to his first Major League Baseball game. My friend was attending his last.

It was a bittersweet evening in Atlanta. We both knew I'd be leaving in the morning and we'd never see each other again. But the closest he came to lamenting his condition was to comment – in a voice that fairly dripped with rue I'm sure he couldn't hear – that the young Miami pitcher, a rookie, was "gonna be a beauty."

He's right. Jose Fernandez is gonna be a beauty. But it's a beauty Silk will never see. And, for the first time in sixty years, his beloved Yankees[2] will have to manage a season without his moral support. As will I.

So what does this have to do with you? The bridge.

A lot of you are planning to cross some bridge "when you get to it."

Silk's story is not about cancer. It's not even about friendship. If I thought you were stupid enough not to realize how hard you should be working to nurture and support the people who love you, I wouldn't think you were smart enough to benefit from a tale about friendship.

No, this story is about bridges. It's about the fallacy involved in crossing that bridge when we get to it. It's about the fact you have to start getting ready to cross the bridges in your life *long before* you get to them.

I've lost 35 pounds since Silk's cancer was diagnosed. That was one bridge I had been expecting to cross when I got to it. I've got lots of others I have to work on, but that was the most obvious.

I don't know what yours is. It might be medical. I have one friend dying and one flying all over the country to see miracle-working shamans – both because they neglected medical attention for something. I have a friend who's an alcoholic and several who are smokers.

Or it might be lifestyle. Our profession has frightening alcoholism and suicide rates. Heart attacks are as common as quarters. We all keep promising ourselves we'll slow down or learn to deal with the stress or take on some help or retire. And we all keep going to the funerals of lawyers who didn't.

---

2   I never said he was perfect.

But he was born in Mickey Mantle's hometown (a wide spot in the road in Oklahoma) on Mickey Mantle's birthday; I figured I had to give him a pass on the Yankee thing.

It might be something I haven't even thought of. If you're reading this in California, you probably know me well enough to know how faulty my thought processes can be. My failure to foresee your personal bridge will probably not surprise you. So don't let the fact I haven't described it keep you from recognizing it as a bridge.

And no matter *what* it is, no matter *where* it is, no matter when you *think* it's going to show up, start preparing for it *now*. Because it's too late when it suddenly looms up on your horizon.

You never met Thomas Gary Wilkinson (1947-2014), but you can profit from his example. If you don't, trust me, you'll remember what he said. And you'll feel pretty stupid when you actually get to the goddam bridge.

CPSIA information can be obtained at www.ICGtesting.com
Printed in the USA
BVOW06s0859030116

431629BV00003B/14/P